T0209032

Surviving a Biblical Childhood

How I Came to Love God in Spite of the Bible

Elizabeth Limkemann

BALBOA.PRESS

A DIVISION OF HAY HOUSE

Balboa Press books may be ordered through booksellers or by contacting:

Balboa Press
A Division of Hay House
1663 Liberty Drive
Bloomington, IN 47403
www.balboapress.com
844-682-1282

Print information available on the last page.

ISBN: 978-1-9822-6481-9 (sc)
ISBN: 978-1-9822-6482-6 (hc)
ISBN: 978-1-9822-6483-3 (e)

Library of Congress Control Number: 2021904064

Balboa Press rev. date: 03/10/2021

In memory of Jake and Verna Limkemann,
who were ideal parents for me, even though
I did not always appreciate them.

And to anyone who has questioned the Bible.

CONTENTS

Preface xi

Chronology xv

Chapter 1   Early Memories..1

Chapter 2   My Parents...7

Chapter 3   Becoming a Missionary......................................17

Chapter 4   Solitary Confinement...23

Chapter 5   Learning about God 27

Chapter 6   Other Stories 31

Chapter 7   A New Baby 33

Chapter 8   How a Pair of Overalls Made Me a Skeptic....37

Chapter 9   A Beautiful Baby 39

Chapter 10   First Grade...41

Chapter 11   The Panama Canal Zone 49

Chapter 12   Music in Our Family 51

Chapter 13   The Executive Director 55

Chapter 14   The Bible House 57

Chapter 15   Church 61

Chapter 16   What I Learned in Sunday School 67

Chapter 17   Testing the Faith...71

Chapter 18   Vacation Bible School 75

Chapter 19   Unanswered Questions 79

Chapter 20   My Child's Eye View of Heaven........................81

Chapter 21   Defending against God.......................................85

Chapter 22   Live Happily Ever After 87

Chapter 23   Learning about Sex...89

Chapter 24   A New Idea to Ponder..93

Chapter 25   My First Bra 95

Chapter 26   Menstruation 103

Chapter 27   Women 107

Chapter 28   A Day in the Limkemann Home 111

Chapter 29 Mealtimes...115
Chapter 30 Dad..119
Chapter 31 Getting Saved...123
Chapter 32 Summer with Grandma...127
Chapter 33 A Welcome Discovery..131
Chapter 34 Teenage Christian...135
Chapter 35 Going to College...141
Chapter 36 Badgered into Getting Saved—Again! 145
Chapter 37 Terry..151
Chapter 38 Dad's Illness..153
Chapter 39 My Father's Legacy...155
Chapter 40 Marriage...159
Chapter 41 Joining the Lutheran Church....................................161
Chapter 42 A Big Decision...163
Chapter 43 Mountain Climbing...167
Chapter 44 Thailand...169
Chapter 45 My Daughters..173
Chapter 46 Unity...175
Chapter 47 Changing My Diet..177
Chapter 48 Teaching Piano Lessons 181
Chapter 49 Yoga..185
Chapter 50 Going to Georgia..187
Chapter 51 Matthew...189
Chapter 52 Divorce..191
Chapter 53 Jay..195
Chapter 54 Rescued by the Church..199
Chapter 55 Inside Essence..201
Chapter 56 Blessings 207
Chapter 57 An Unexpected Benefit..209
Chapter 58 Death of John Matthews..213
Chapter 59 My Career Finds Me..215
Chapter 60 What I Like about Church 223
Chapter 61 Getting Mom off My Back 225
Chapter 62 Beginning Sahaj Marg Spiritual Practice....................227
Chapter 63 India...231

Chapter 64 Leaving Sahaj Marg 235

Chapter 65 Thoughts about the Bible 237

Chapter 66 Jesus 241

Chapter 67 What Is in the Bible? 243

Chapter 68 Good and Evil in the Bible 245

Chapter 69 More about Righteousness 247

Chapter 70 Questioning the Inspiration of the Bible 249

Chapter 71 More Questions about the Bible 253

Chapter 72 What Is Wrong with Me? 255

Chapter 73 Alternative Versions of the Bible 257

Chapter 74 Finding My Way, Again 261

Chapter 75 Getting Over the Bible 263

Chapter 76 Goodbye to Big, Bad, Scary God 267

Chapter 77 A Course in Miracles 271

Chapter 78 God Did Not Create This World 275

Chapter 79 The Message of A Course in Miracles 279

PREFACE

Why I Wanted to Write My Story

ALTHOUGH FEWER AND FEWER PEOPLE in the world identify themselves as Christians, the Bible is still well known and continues to have enormous influence on the thoughts and ideas of Western civilization. Its influence is very evident in language, literature, art, movies, and music, and in many laws and customs. There are millions of Bibles in print, in over two thousand languages. There are Gideon Bibles in hotel rooms. People are asked to swear on the Bible in courtrooms. Bible courses are taught in many colleges and universities, and there are plenty of printed and online Bible study courses. And of course the Bible is still taught and proclaimed in the many churches that are still in existence.

Although the Bible is considered to be "holy" and "the word of God," there are many ideas in the Bible that are inconsistent with high ideals and many stories that lead to questionable conclusions. And the way God is portrayed, especially in the Old Testament, can hardly be said to inspire love and trust.

Having grown up with daily exposure to Bible reading by parents who deeply venerated that book, I have had ample opportunity to consider the teachings of the Bible and interpret them in my own way. Many of the discomforts and fears of my childhood were directly related to ways the Bible was used and the ways I thought about it. As a child, I thought that I was the only person who had problems with the Bible, while everyone else thought that the Bible was wonderful and true. And even as an adult, I have rarely encountered others who were willing to look at the seamy side, the inconsistencies, or the horrors of the Bible.

For years, I have been looking for a book that questions the Bible in the ways that I have doubted it and often despised it. I have not found any to completely satisfy me. And I rarely find stories of people who became disenchanted with biblical religion and found their way to a broader form of spirituality. So I have taken this advice, attributed to

Toni Morrison: "If there's a book you really want to read and it hasn't been written yet, then you must write it."

I have read stories of people who overcame harsh religious training and found their way to a more encompassing form of Christianity. I Fired God by Jocelyn Zichterman tells how she escaped from an extremely repressive Christian cult and "fired" the God of hellfire, brimstone, and damnation to replace Him with a loving, kind, and compassionate God in a more liberal church. Sue Monk Kidd, in The Dance of the Dissident Daughter and When the Heart Waits, poses legitimate questions about faith, especially in regard to women's issues and still remains true to her Christian foundation. Their answers apparently work for them, but my questions about God and the Bible demand more radical and complete answers.

I have found a number of books that tell stories of people giving up religion for atheism. I loved An Unquenchable Thirst, in which Mary Johnson tells of her struggles as one of Mother Teresa's nuns for twenty years and how she eventually forsakes her vows to become an atheist. Dan Barker relates his passage from enthusiastic evangelical preacher to atheist in Losing Faith in Faith. Ruth Hurmence Green goes into detail about the cruelties of the God of the Bible in The Born Again Skeptic's Guide to the Bible. She also tells of her journey from Methodist to atheist. Charles Templeton's story in Farewell to God details his journey from being a famous evangelist (in the same league as Billy Graham) to becoming an atheist.

I respect their choices, but I know that atheism is not the path for me. Although I did not want to accept the harsh, punitive God I had been exposed to, I did not give up my search for a god I could love.

One day when I was fourteen, I was suddenly struck with an amazing thought: If God loves everyone, then God loves Catholics and Jews and Muslims and Hindus and even atheists! Although I had to hold this thought privately as long as I lived in the home of my Protestant Bible-reading parents, I had a way of knowing that the real truth was much greater than what I was being taught. Somehow I clung to the idea that there was a God somewhere who was not vengeful and prejudiced like the God of the Bible as I understood it.

Books by John Shelby Spong, especially The Sins of the Scripture, help me to feel supported in my horror and dismay about many aspects of the Bible. As deep-thinking and as far-reaching as Bishop Spong and others have been, they have not quite gotten to the root of my most basic questions. Why were those particular writings chosen to be included in Sacred Scripture? Why have so many people given so much authority to the Bible in spite of all the contradictions and injustices and violence contained in it? How did the Bible come to be such an important and influential book?

Recently, I heard about the early New Haven Colony, where they had no laws except those found in the Bible, as it was interpreted by clergymen who studied the Bible. They didn't even have trial by jury, because juries were not mentioned in the Bible. That is one extreme example among countless ways the Bible has been used and abused.

I am aware that disenchantment with Christianity is widespread. There are hordes of nonpracticing Catholics and plenty of Protestants who are no longer involved with a church. And most of them seem to be satisfied to remain in religious limbo. That has not been my way. When I decided that I did not want to consider myself a Christian, I started on a long search for something better and kept looking until I found it. Here is my story of the influence the Bible had on me as a child, the strategies I used to deal with the effects of the Bible, and how I eventually found satisfactory answers to my questions.

CHRONOLOGY

1850–1890. Most of my ancestors emigrate from Germany to Illinois

1908. My father, Jacob Limkemann, is born

1915. My mother, Verna Peters, is born

1934. My parents marry

1938. Jake and Verna go to Honduras

1940. My brother, Will, is born

1943. Jake, Verna, and Will return to the United States of America

1944, July. I am born

1944, September. We go to Honduras

1947. My sister Ruth is born

1949. We return to the United States and go to Princeton, New Jersey

1949. My sister Eunice is born

1950. We stay with Uncle Ed in Illinois

1951. We move to the Panama Canal Zone

1955. We return to Princeton, New Jersey

1956. We return to the Panama Canal Zone

1961. I graduate from high school and go to College of Wooster, Ohio

1966. I marry Terry Miller

1967. We move to Indiana, where Terry studies at Indiana University

1969. Terry is drafted and sent to Vietnam

1970. Our daughter Sonia is born, and Terry returns from Vietnam

1973. Terry, Sonia, and I spend a year in Thailand

1974. We live with Terry's parents in Dover, Ohio

1975. Our daughter Esther is born

1976. Terry starts teaching at Kent State University, Kent, Ohio, and we move to Kent

1979. I begin to study A Course in Miracles

1984. Terry and I divorce

1985. I marry Fred and move to North Carolina

1990. I move back to Ohio and get divorced again

1994. I move to Connecticut

1999. I begin my practice of Sahaj Marg meditation

2017. I end my practice of Sahaj Marg

2020. I rediscover A Course in Miracles

CHAPTER 1

Early Memories

Comayaguela, Honduras, 1947

Will and me with parakeet

MY PARENTS NAMED ME ELIZABETH Ann, but they call me Betty. I'm three years old. I'm little, and I have brown eyes and brown curly hair. I don't smile very much. I have dimples in my elbows and in my little hands. When I put my leg out straight, my knee looks like a poached egg. I wear little white or pink dresses and white shoes and socks—and, of course, panties.

I have to wear panties all the time, but I'm not supposed to let anyone see them. It's really hard to not let my panties show. I have to stand up or sit down very carefully. A lot of times I forget and sit on the floor, letting my panties show. Mommy tells me and tells me, "Don't let your panties show."

I get very tired of being so careful. I think I can hardly ever please my parents. But I don't know any other way to live—this is the way it has always been for me, and I guess it will be like this until I grow up. Someday I will be grown up and will have more freedom, but that is a very long way off.

This is our house. When you come in the big wooden front door, first there is a dark hall. When you walk to the right, there is a bench by the wall, and two wicker chairs by the edge of the courtyard. Sometimes I play in the courtyard. That's where the rabbit hutch is. I like to pick up the soft furry rabbits. They feel so soft and warm, and I have a sweet, happy feeling when I hold them. I like to hold the baby rabbits up to their mother when they drink her milk. Also, sometimes I taste the plants growing in the courtyard. There is one plant with sour leaves that I like.

My room is near the corner, past the bench. There are two beds in my room, even though my brother, Will, doesn't sleep here anymore. He is seven years old, and he has gone to the boarding school for missionary children in Huehuetanango. That's in Guatemala. We live in Honduras.

Mommy and Daddy sleep in the bedroom in the corner. There is a window in their room. Sometimes I look out the window and see children playing. The children run around barefoot. Mommy says it's not proper for me to be barefoot. The Honduran children speak Spanish. Some of them don't wear any clothes. They are dirty, too. I have to stay clean, or Mommy gets mad.

Mommy and Daddy keep their clothes in that chest of drawers. Once, I was out in the hall and I looked through the keyhole when Daddy was getting dressed. He put on his trousers over his underwear, and he put his belt through the belt loops. I had never seen Daddy's underwear before, and I didn't know how he put his belt through the belt loops. Mommy and Daddy don't want me to see them getting dressed; that's why they close the door. But I can look through the keyhole.

I like doing things I'm not supposed to do, unless I get caught! Besides, I really want to know what people look like without their clothes. I always undress my dolls, but they don't have real body parts like people.

Sometimes Daddy holds my hand and skips with me. I really like that! Sometimes he gives me piggyback rides, and sometimes he lets me sit on his lap. And sometimes he sings with me or tells me stories. I really like when he pays attention to me, but usually he is out talking to people. Sometimes he gets on the mule and goes away for a few days.

Around the corner is the living room. There is a table with a kerosene lamp on it and a few chairs. Sometimes the grown-ups sit in here and read after they put me to bed. I don't know how to read, so I like it when someone reads to me. I especially like the book about Peter Rabbit. It's an exciting story. Even though I've heard it before, I like to hear about Peter's adventures. And I like how his mother takes good care of him even after he got in trouble.

The last room on this side is the kitchen, where Mommy cooks meals and washes dishes. There is a big black stove. It is hot. I try to be careful not to touch it. They put wood in it and make a fire. Mommy has two irons that she heats on the stove. When one is hot enough, she has a wooden handle that she puts on so she can iron clothes. She wants me to keep my clothes clean because washing and ironing is hard work. I try very hard to stay clean, but sometimes my clothes get dirty; I don't even know how.

Now, if we go back to the door from the street and turn the other way, we come to the chapel. When people come for services, Mommy plays hymns on the pump organ. She sits there, pushing the black pedals up and down, and the sweet sound of hymns comes out as she moves her fingers around on the white and black keys. People sing along. Daddy sings, too, and he reads from his Spanish Bible, and he talks in Spanish. He talks a long time.

I have to sit still and be quiet, even when it is long and boring. Sometimes Mommy gives me her handkerchief to play with. The people who come to services sit on the chairs that are set up in the chapel. Usually it's all grown-ups. I would like to play with children, but I feel very shy with Honduran children. I don't know very much Spanish. Besides, Mommy won't let me play with Honduran children. And there aren't any other children around, so I have to play by myself, which is not much fun.

The room in the corner is where Chicha sleeps. Chicha is a big girl, almost a woman. Her parents died, so she lives with us. She helps Mommy do her work. Sometimes she takes care of me. There is a curtain instead of a door at Chicha's room. She has her own bed and a dresser for her clothes.

The bathroom is next. When I sit on the toilet, my feet don't touch the floor. Once I forgot to close the bathroom door, and Mommy went past and said, "Oh, look at Queen Esther sitting on her throne!"

I felt really embarrassed. Since then, I always try to remember to close the bathroom door.

At the other end of our house is the laundry room and clotheslines. Mommy and Chicha wash our clothes with a washboard, scrubbing up and down, up and down, and then rinsing in water and twisting them to get out the water. I have my own little washboard, and I wash my doll clothes and sometimes handkerchiefs. The soap has a strong smell. Sometimes I spill water on the floor. I don't mean to; it just splashes out of the washtub.

Mommy and Chicha keep washing clothes for a long time, but I get tired of washing. I want to play, except I don't know what to do. I can go play with my dolls, but I get tired of playing with them. Sometimes I twirl around and around until I get so dizzy I fall down, and even after I fall down on the floor, it looks like the room is spinning around. That's fun to do once or twice—I like to get dizzy, but I don't like to stay dizzy.

Mommy likes to read to me from Hurlbut's Bible stories for children. I like the story of the little children going to see Jesus and sitting on his lap.

I ask Mommy, "Where is Jesus?"

She says, "Jesus is up in heaven, with God."

"Mommy, what does God look like?"

"God is invisible."

"What does that mean?"

"That means you can't see Him."

I ask, "Is there a Mrs. God?"

"No."

"Why not?"

"I don't know. That's just the way it is."

"What does God do?"

"God is always watching us."

"Can we see God watching us?"

"No. God is invisible."

I'm thinking maybe God isn't really invisible. Maybe we just can't see him because He's watching us from behind. Maybe if I turn around really, really fast, I'll surprise God and catch Him watching me before he can get behind me again. For several days, whenever I think of it, I turn around really, really fast, hoping that I'll catch God watching me. Then I'll know what God looks like! But I never see God. Maybe God can move faster than I can turn around.

My mother tells me that I must never ever touch myself down there. I don't really know why. Once when I was sick, she gave me an enema. I didn't like it. I cried and fussed. I didn't like lying on a rubber sheet and having her put that thing in my bottom. And I didn't like making lots of watery poo-poo. But having an enema gave me an exciting fizzy slippery feeling down there. I like having that feeling! I wonder why all the grownups around me seem to not be interested in having good feelings down there. I promise myself that, when I grow up, I will still like to have good feelings down there. And I won't forget what it's like to be a child. When I grow up, I will be nice to my children. I won't scold them and punish them all the time, and I will let them play and get dirty. I'm promising this to my grown-up self, and I promise not to forget.

One day, Mommy says Don Simon is going to be coming to stay with us for a few days. I am not happy to hear that. When my parents have company, they pay attention to their company, and they want me to be quiet while the grown-ups talk to each other.

I ask, "Who is Don Simon?"

"He's a pastor from Las Colinas, and he's a friend of your father."

"Does he have any children?"

"No. He's not married."

"Mommy, why do people get married before they have children."

"That's just the way it is. You'll understand when you're older."

"Where is Don Simon going to sleep?"

"We'll set up a cot for him in the living room. While he's here, I want you to be especially good. Don't interrupt people when they're talking, and make sure you shut the bathroom door when you're in there, and don't let your panties show."

"If I don't wear any panties, they won't show," I say mischievously.

Mommy, disapprovingly: "You must never let people see you down there. And if you talk any more about not wearing panties, you'll get your mouth washed out with soap."

"Mommy, can you read to me?"

"Okay. Come and sit beside me."

"I want to sit on your lap."

"I don't have much of a lap. Just sit beside me."

"Mommy, why do you have such a big tummy?"

Mommy, in a tone of voice that means she won't talk about it: "Oh, I don't know. Would you like me to read The Tale of Peter Rabbit?"

I say okay and sigh and suck my thumb.

I like it when she reads to me, but I wish I could sit on her lap and snuggle with her.

CHAPTER 2

My Parents

WHAT WERE MY PARENTS DOING in Honduras? What had persuaded them to leave friends and family to journey to a distant land where they would live with a language and a culture and people unfamiliar to them? Knowing about their backgrounds might offer some clues about why they went and the beliefs and practices they took with them.

My father, Jacob, was the youngest of five children in an Illinois farm family. They all worked hard during the week, even young Jake, whose chores included feeding chickens and pigs and weeding the vegetable garden. On Sunday, they were always the first family to arrive at the small church, whether they traveled in a horse-drawn wagon or, later, an automobile. People said that his mother, Lydia, was the kind of person who would wash tomorrow's dishes today if she could.

Nobody in Jake's family had any education beyond a few years of elementary school. Jake was so hungry for education that, after completing the eighth grade in a one-room schoolhouse (grades one through eight in one room) he took eighth grade again, because he didn't think any other educational opportunities would be available to him. He then found a way to go to the nearest high school, eight miles away. He rode a horse from the family farm on Monday morning and then turned the horse loose to find its own way home. He stayed in town with a family during the week and then returned home for the weekend. I think he may have walked home on Friday, or when he was on the track team, he ran part of the way home rather than stay after school for track practice.

After completing high school, he was able to study at Wheaton College, where he waited tables and did other work to put himself through school. Wheaton College in Wheaton Illinois was, and still is, a very conservative evangelical Christian college with high academic as well as moral standards. I know very little about Dad's college days, but I have seen a picture that won a college prize—he (Jacob) with his friend Isaac standing behind a picture of Abraham Lincoln. The caption reads, "Abraham, Isaac and Jacob" (as in the biblical patriarchs). This shows ingenuity as well as a sense of humor.

Another snippet I have from his college days is an excerpt from an essay he wrote after Christmas vacation:

> Some rather queer things happen in almost every vacation. When Father found me way back on the bales in the old cow barn, reading a book, I suppose he thought that strange. Why should anyone want to read in a barn when he could just as well be in a house? Aw, well! one can be in a house any of the three hundred and sixty days of the year but how often can one find a snug nook in a cozy barn next to a window with fancy cobwebs for curtains and the sun for heating and lighting? Such environment should warm the coldest, and soften the hardest heart.

Chemistry was his major; he had wanted to become a doctor but eventually decided that the cost of medical school was out of his reach. As he had a strong Christian faith since childhood, it was quite natural for him to choose the ministry as his profession. It proved to be a good choice for him; he was consistently enthusiastic and avidly interested in Christianity for the rest of his life.

My mother's father, Okko Benjamin Peters, was the country preacher in that small, close-knit community. He had moved his family to Sutter, Illinois, when my mother was just nine years old. One of the local teenagers who helped them move into their house was sixteen-year-old Jake Limkemann. My mother, Verna Peters, thought that Limkemann was the strangest name she had ever heard, never dreaming that someday it would be her name.

Okko and Mary Alice (Ward) Peters would gather their eight children at mealtimes to sit through lengthy prayers before eating could begin. After the meal, Okko would read from the Bible, with all the children held captive. Then he would ask for the "little sticks," which was what he called toothpicks. Once Verna and one of her sisters, with their mother's permission, collected some small twigs and passed them to their father when he asked for little sticks. He laughed, enjoying the moment with his family. However, most of the time Okko and Mary Alice were stern and strict, making sure their children behaved well and kept up with schoolwork and family chores, such as milking the cow and shelling peas.

Religion was the guiding force for both families. Theirs was a somber, zealous form of conservative Protestant Christianity. I have tried to understand what they believed and what forces shaped their beliefs and practices.

The ancestors of most of the people in the community had come from Germany, where the German Reformed Church had been oppressed and its members persecuted, especially by Catholic political and religious leaders. A primary reason for many immigrants coming to America was the freedom to practice their religion without fear.

The beliefs of the German Reformed Church are outlined in the Heidelberg Catechism, which affirms that our duty is to love the Lord our God with all our heart, soul, and mind, but we are unable to do that because of our sinful nature, which was passed on to all humans from Adam and Eve. We need to be born again by the Spirit of God. But God is very angry with us for sinning and will punish us now and in eternity, so we need a mediator who is true God and true man. Jesus is that mediator. And if we have true faith and wholehearted trust, we will have forgiveness of our sins and eternal righteousness and salvation. This is what was taught in the small church that both my parents attended as children.

In 1931, Jake began studying for the ministry at Dallas Theological Seminary in Texas. The following year, he returned home to help out on the farm during his father's illness. While at home, he started courting Verna. After his father's death, he returned to seminary in 1933.

Verna and Jake's wedding picture

Verna and Jake were married in August 1934. On the morning of their wedding day, they went in to town to have a photographer take their wedding picture, a full-length picture of a man and a young woman, both well dressed and both looking very serious. Verna's chin-length brown hair is arranged in careful waves around her face. Her eyes are serious, even a little distant, and she is not wearing glasses, which will soon be her constant facial accessory. She has brought her chin forward, as was her longtime custom, so as to minimize her overbite. She is wearing a string of white beads around her slender neck, and she is holding a large bouquet of flowers at waist level in front of her new two-piece dress. The hem of her dress reaches nearly to her ankles, and although her feet are turned slightly toward Jake, her face is turned slightly away. She is wearing white pumps that look too wide on her narrow feet. (They remind me of Minnie Mouse.) Jake is wearing a dark well-pressed suit, a white shirt, and a light-colored necktie. There is a flower in his lapel. His fine hair is well trimmed (his mother was exceptionally skilled at cutting men's hair). He is turned slightly toward Verna, exposing one of his large, prominent ears. His hands are behind his back. The most striking aspect of the picture is the distance between them. They appear to be standing about a foot apart.

Once my sisters and I were sitting in the living room with Mom, and we asked Mom about their wedding. She told us, "I bought a blue dress for my wedding dress. In those days, we didn't have much money, so I chose a dress that I could use for other occasions after the wedding."

Eunice asked, "Was it a long dress, down to your feet?"

"No," said Mom. "It was just a regular street-length dress. The morning of our wedding day, Dad and I went in to town and had our wedding picture taken. We were married at home, with only our families there—your father's mother and brothers and sister and their families were all there, and my sisters, including Aunt Mildred's husband, Bill, and their little boy. My brothers had gone to town to buy ice for the ice cream we would make and serve later. Aunt Hester played the wedding march on the piano."

Ruth: "Was Aunt Hester as fat as she is now?"

Mom: "She was always quite plump, but she has gotten much heavier since then.

"After we were married by my father, everyone sat down to a delicious dinner, which my mother had prepared. Two of my friends helped serve the meal."

I asked, "Did you have a wedding cake?"

Mom: "Yes. My friend Fern Miller Scheurman made the cake.

"Later that evening a lot of people came around for the charivari" (she pronounced it /shiverEE/ and told us it was the custom in that area for well-wishers to come around banging on pots and pans as a serenade to a newly married couple). "We served homemade ice cream to over two hundred people. Then your father and I spent the night at my parents' house."

I asked, incredulously, "You spent your wedding night at your parents' house?"

Mom said, "We had nothing to hide."

The way she said that and also knowing how shy and modest she still was, I got the idea that they did not consummate the marriage right away. I also noticed one time when Dad mentioned a particular month and day to Mom, and she blushed and said, "Oh Jake," trying to brush aside his teasing.

Of course, I don't know the intimate details of the start of their marriage, but I like to imagine it was something like this:

On their wedding night, Verna undresses behind the closet door and puts on her new white nightgown and panties. Jake modestly takes off his clothes behind the closet door and puts on his pajamas, even though it is a warm August night. He kisses her and gets into bed beside her. He says, "Are you ready, Verna?"

She says, "Yes. I'm ready to sleep beside you. It has been a long day."

He starts to pull up the hem of her nightgown, and she pulls away, saying, "What are you doing?"

He says, "It's our wedding night."

She says, "Yes it is, and I'm happy to be your wife. I'll sleep on this side of the bed, and you sleep on that side."

Over the next few days, when she continues to resist his advances, Jake realizes that Verna doesn't know about the physical side of marriage. She has never been told, has never figured it out, and she is extremely modest and protective about her body. He says, "Uh, Verna, do you know how babies are made?"

She says, "They grow inside the mother's stomach."

"Do you know how they get there?"

"Well, no."

He then tries to tell her what couples do to conceive a child, and she says, "I can't believe that. My mother has had eight children, and she's a very proper lady.

I'm sure she never did that. There must be another way to have children without doing something so disgusting."

After they have moved into their little apartment near Dallas Theological Seminary and Verna continues to be unconvinced, Jake confides in his New Testament professor, Henry Jones. "My dear young wife doesn't know what a man and his wife are supposed to do in bed. I told her about it, and she thinks it's disgusting. What can I do to persuade her to be my wife in body as well as in spirit?"

The professor considers the problem, and then he suggests, "I'll see if my wife would be willing to talk to her."

A few days later, Verna and Jake are invited to dinner at the professor's house. After dinner, Jake and Mr. Jones retire to another room, and Verna and Mary Jones (who is nursing their baby) are still sitting at the table. Verna, blushing, says, "Jake has been trying to tell me that the way married couples make babies is to put their private parts together. Is that really true?"

Mary Jones tells her, "I wondered about that before I was married. I knew that the Bible says that God created us male and female, so there must be a good reason for God to create two sexes. When the Bible says that Adam knew his wife and she bore a son, it means that they had sexual intercourse together. Do you know what that is?"

Verna shakes her head. "Not really."

"Well, let me tell you. Normally a man's member hangs down, loose and relaxed. But when he gets aroused with desire for his wife, it becomes stiff and able to enter the opening in the woman's body. It's the same opening where blood comes out during your time of the month."

"I can't believe that. Isn't it messy? Doesn't it get all bloody?"

"Well it is a little messy. Couples usually avoid doing it during the woman's monthly period when it would be especially messy. Once the wife gets used to it, she often enjoys it as a natural gift from God. And by having this intimate pleasure together, a strong bond develops between husband and wife. So you see, it's not just for the purpose of having children. It also helps the couple to be loving partners with each other."

Verna responds, "When my mother told me that it is a wife's duty to submit to her husband, I didn't really know what she meant. And I still can't believe that people do that and even enjoy it."

After contemplating this new information for a few days, Verna agrees to try it. Even though Jake is gentle and tender, Verna does not enjoy it. But she understands that it is her duty, and she really wants to be a good wife in every possible way. She eventually gets used to the idea of sexual intercourse, but she never develops enthusiasm for it.

They were an idealistic young couple. Jake worked hard at his studies so that he could become the best minister he could be, and Verna tried to follow her mother's example to be a good minister's wife, which meant playing hymns on the piano, teaching Sunday School classes, entertaining guests, and keeping a thrifty and tidy home so that her husband's energies could be directed toward his important work.

Jake and Verna had counted the money they had earned from their summer jobs, divided it by the number of weeks in the school year, and discovered that they would have five dollars a week for rent and four dollars for everything else. Verna was well trained in the arts of frugal homemaking. She washed their clothes by hand, did all her own sewing and mending, and prepared tasty meals with the least expensive ingredients. They ate large quantities of grapefruit and spinach, and they had meat only once a week.

They often had guests for their special meal of the week, usually one of Jake's seminary friends, along with the friend's wife, if he was married. All through their married life, they entertained guests frequently. And Verna was adept at making these meals special, with a tablecloth, fine china (which they had received as a wedding gift), flowers on the table, and specially prepared food. I remember "company dinners" when I was growing up, with generous platters of meat, bowls of vegetables and salad, and always a special dessert. Occasionally, she would astonish family and friends with baked Alaska—a slab of ice cream on top of a rectangle of sponge cake, covered with sweetened meringue and baked in a hot oven. The cake and meringue insulated the ice cream well enough that it was still frozen even though the rest of the dessert was hot.

Occasionally Jake would show up with an impromptu guest at noon, telling Verna to add another cup of water to the soup. She would deftly find a way to stretch the meal.

During Jake's final year at seminary, Verna was able to supplement their finances occasionally by doing some typing or sewing, and Jake was occasionally paid for preaching at a church when the pastor was away. Most of the people around them were also on very tight budgets; even the faculty at the seminary had to endure pay cuts during those difficult times, so Verna and Jake's frugal standard of living was similar to that of many people around them.

CHAPTER 3

Becoming a Missionary

Iowa to Honduras, 1935–1940

AFTER GRADUATING FROM SEMINARY IN 1935, Jake served as pastor of a church in Stacyville, Iowa, for a year and a half. While he was there, he met a few people who were serving as missionaries to Central America. He began to feel a great desire to become a missionary.

He had many reasons to want to be a missionary. He deeply believed in the words of Jesus: "I am the way and the truth and the life. No man comes to the Father except through Me" (John 14:6). And "Go ye into all the world and preach the gospel to every creature" (Mark 16:15). He yearned to speak to people who had not had the opportunity to hear the Gospel, and he considered it his duty, as well as his joy, to save the souls of as many people as he could. He knew that, in America, most people were at least aware of Christianity, and so they had the opportunity to accept Jesus Christ as their Savior if they so chose. He also knew that, in other countries, there were many unsaved souls who had not had the privilege of hearing the Gospel.

There was an urgency to his mission. He believed, as did members of the Central American Mission board, that Christ would come again and that it would happen by the year 2000, a doctrine that they called premillennialism. They based that idea on their interpretation of Revelations 20, which makes reference to the end of a thousand years. And if Jesus was going to come again before 2000, there was not much time left to save souls.

He first applied to the Presbyterian Mission and was rejected because of "lack of initiative and leadership." Jake took that as a challenge and proved, in future years, that he did indeed have initiative and leadership.

In 1938, the Central American Mission board approved him as a missionary and assigned him to Santa Barbara in Honduras. Their home church pledged to support them financially in spite of the fact that many people were experiencing financial hardship.

In order to get a passport to travel to Honduras, Jake needed to show his birth certificate. This was a problem. His birth at home in 1908 had never been officially recorded. By taking his mother and older brother to the county courthouse to verify his place and date of birth, he was able to get a birth certificate.

My mother tells of their journey: "We sailed from New Orleans on the Santa Marta, a United Fruit Company ship. After a few days at sea, we arrived in Puerto Barrios, Guatemala, our first stop, where we first set foot on Central American soil. It was October 1, 1938, Jake's thirtieth birthday. He had made the remark that he wanted to begin his life work at age thirty. We were not greatly impressed with what we saw. It was the rainy season, and it was raining and muddy. Jake described it in his journal as a 'low-lying, feverish little village with cows tied here and there. Trees were, it seemed to me, to be full of buzzards. These were ugly birds, but very beneficial to the tropical countries, for they eat garbage and dead animals.'"

After a terrifying truck ride over several mountains of Honduras, they settled in Tegucigalpa, the capital of Honduras, where their first order of business was to study Spanish. My mother's name, Verna, was acceptable in Spanish, but my father's first name, Jacob, presented difficulties. So he adopted the Spanish form of his middle name, William (Guillermo).

Jake riding a mule

A few months after arriving in Honduras, Jake had an opportunity to visit Santa Barbara with a local Honduran pastor. Although he was not yet fluent in the language, he was eager to be introduced to the area where he would be working. They traveled for several days on mule back over mountains and through marshes, hanging their hammocks in the homes of hospitable strangers at night. Jake made note of the poverty he saw, and rejoiced in the natural beauty of some of the landscapes and birds and flowers. As they passed through towns and villages where there were no believers (that is to say, no persons who had accepted Jesus Christ as their savior) he saw the potential and the need for mission work.

He also was privileged to spend time in Colinas, where a lone missionary had done exemplary work previously. He wrote in a letter to the pastor of his home church:

> A thrill of joy surges through my soul as I think that now I am in the center of the scenes of labor of Miss Anna Gohrman who came here in the year 1913. She labored 13 years then rested from her labors. All we see of spiritual light and life in this whole section can be traced back chiefly to her. Others have entered since and carried on nobly. While I was in seminary I heard Dr. Chafer speak of Miss Gohrman as an example of a house-to-house evangelist. He said that she went all through these hills from house to house with the gospel. I little dreamt at that time that I would ever be where she so zealously carried on. Believers and unbelievers all remember Miss Gohrman, not only in Colinas, but all around here—even in Santa Barbara, but in the latter town no work seems to have ever been begun.

In 1940 Verna and Jake settled into an adobe house near the central plaza of Santa Barbara, for the purpose of introducing Christianity to people in the town and in the outlying areas. One of their strategies to familiarize the local people with their work was to have family devotions at home, with doors and windows open so that people could see and hear and join them if they wished. Two Honduran lay preachers moved into Santa Barbara soon after they arrived, and the lay preachers helped to expand the mission work.

In July Verna flew to Tegucigalpa (she was the only passenger in a cargo plane) to await the birth of their first child, my brother, William, who arrived on September 1.

With the help of several lay preachers and occasional visits from a Honduran minister and several missionaries, the number of believers grew beyond the capacity of the small chapel in Jake and Verna's house. The mission encouraged them to rent a larger chapel, where they held Sunday services, Sunday school, and midweek prayer meetings. In addition, they kept an open reading room in their house, where people could come and read the Bible and other literature.

Verna taught some people to read, as many were illiterate. By the mid-1940s, the Honduran government had launched a literacy program, encouraged by Dr. Frank Laubach, an internationally known literacy specialist whose motto was, "Each one teach one." Some of the Christian converts who had learned to read in order to read the Bible were able to teach others to read.

In 1941, after much reading and thinking, my father began to have doubts about premillennialism. He wrote a letter to Mr. Hummel of the mission board saying, "I am very much aware that it is stated that when one finds that he cannot subscribe in toto to the Statement of Faith, he should hold himself in readiness to terminate his relation with the mission. My concern is that the Lord's work suffer no setback … We trust that we may be allowed to continue for the present, at least."

Mr. Hummel replied, "I must confess that I am concerned and burdened that a doctrinal matter should now come in to take even our time and thought—when the previous outlook for your work and ministry in Honduras had been so bright and hopeful … Article 6 of the Doctrinal Statement commits us to the premillennial position. Have you had doubts through these past years as to the premillennial position? If not, then may I ask after whom you have been reading?"

My father replied that his change of belief had been gradual over the years, as he read the writings of various thinkers and "endeavored to compare their teaching with the Scriptures."

In March 1943, he resigned from the mission and returned to the United States of America. The work in Santa Barbara continued, with the help of local lay preachers, and eventually, the daughter of my father's cousin and her husband (Lee and Mildred Irons) took over the missionary work in Santa Barbara.

Back in the United States, Jake became the pastor of a small church in Marion, South Dakota, which was in the process of transitioning from services in both German and English to services exclusively in English. To help those who were not very fluent in English, he started using visual props for Bible stories in the form of a flannelgraph board. He ordered the appropriate illustrations, which came from California on large sheets of paper. Verna painted them with poster paints, cut them out, and glued pieces of flannel to the back, which then adhered easily (and temporarily) to the three-foot-by-four-foot board covered with flannel. This visual prop helped to increase understanding of the Bible stories that he was teaching. In later years, my mother would use the same flannelgraph board in teaching Sunday school. Sometimes, we children would help her paint and cut out figures of bearded men in robes, children in robes, and occasional women with scarves over their hair.

In July 1944 (inconveniently for my father, as it was on a Sunday morning), I was born in a hospital in Sioux Falls. After catching a glimpse of me, his first daughter, my father drove back to Marion in time to teach a Sunday school class. His mother was with us for a few months to help out the household, and even in her seventies she was still hardworking and efficient.

By the time I was born, my father had decided that he could again accept premillennialism, along with the other articles of faith of the Central American Mission. He applied and was accepted again as a missionary, and he returned to Honduras, this time with two children as well as his wife. We lived in Comayaguela in a rented house, which I still remember. Dad returned to his enthusiastic evangelizing, going on frequent trips, often by mule, and nurturing the growing number of Christians in Comayaguela.

At one point, he was invited to teach at a Bible Institute in Guatemala for three months. He declined the invitation, reasoning that it would be easier to find other people to teach than to find another missionary who was willing and able to travel to the areas where he had been working.

Mr. Hummel (from the mission board) encouraged him to go to the Institute: "What I do covet for the young people at the Institute is for you to make a visit there whenever you can for at least some chapel services. The students at our institute need the inspiration of the type of work that you are doing and in which you are so able. If you could impart to the group of students the inspiration and the challenge of the rural areas … it would certainly be worthwhile … I do hope you can visit the school now and again for a brief inspirational ministry."

CHAPTER 4

Solitary Confinement

Comayaguela, Honduras, 1947

WHEN I WAS THREE YEARS old, I stayed almost exclusively inside our house, which was built around a courtyard. I hardly ever went outside, although I sometimes enjoyed the sunshine in the courtyard. On Sundays, my parents opened the heavy door to the outside, and they greeted people as they came in to attend a service in the chapel, where my father read the Bible and preached in Spanish and my mother played hymns on the portable pump organ. There were maybe ten or fifteen men and women who came to the chapel services. I don't remember any children being there. I was expected to sit quietly during the long, boring service.

When my brother Will was home, sometimes he played with me, although he often chose to do things I couldn't do; being four years older he was much bigger and stronger than me. After two years of homeschooling, he was sent, at age seven, to a boarding school in Guatemala for children of missionaries. That left me, three years old, at home with nobody to play with. My father was out most of the time, and my mother was usually busy with her cooking; washing, ironing, and sewing clothes; and keeping the house clean.

Me with my dolls

I had long, long days to try to fill. I played with my dolls. I liked to undress and dress them. I could talk to them and put them to bed in their own doll bed. And sometimes I spanked them if they were bad. Sometimes I had paper

23

and crayons for coloring, and occasionally I had a magazine to cut up with scissors. I spent a great deal of time just hanging around wanting something to do. Time moved very slowly. Every day seemed like an eternity.

I can remember a few occasions when I went outside. Once I went for a walk in the late afternoon with my mother and "Aunt" Mabel Elthon, a visiting missionary who had a loud voice and a big chin. It was cool outside, and I was wearing my sweater. The road was dusty, and my white shoes were getting dirty. We all had really tall shadows. My shadow was so much taller than me. I wanted to talk about that, but the grown-ups were busy talking to each other. I could see that we were walking toward the edge of the world. I was very excited to see what it looked like! Of course I didn't know about the horizon; I really thought we would soon see what there was beyond the edge of the flat world. As we kept walking, the edge of the world kept moving farther away, making a new edge, so I never got to see what was over the edge of the world.

Could not smile for the photographer

Once I was taken to the shop of a professional photographer. Dressed in a pretty white dress, I was seated on a wicker chair and told to smile. The situation was so unfamiliar that I was very uncomfortable, and I was afraid of the photographer, who seemed to be hiding behind a big camera with a black cloth over his head. I found it impossible to smile.

Being accustomed to this drab, uninteresting life, I was happily surprised one day to hear the joyful sound of children playing. I had just put my dolls down for a nap when I heard voices outside the window of my parents' bedroom. I quickly ran into their room and climbed up on the bed so I could look out the window. I saw a group of boys splashing and playing in a puddle in the dirt road beside our house. They were a little older than me, and they were splashing and laughing and chattering happily in Spanish. I had never seen a group of children having so much fun together. I had not known that was even a possibility! I was mesmerized and delighted at the sight. The boys appeared to be having a very good time. They didn't seem to care that they were getting spattered with mud. All were barefoot, and some of the boys were naked. One wore shorts, and another wore a shirt. They didn't seem to care about their clothes; they were just enjoying playing together.

One of the boys saw me looking out the window. He spoke to me and waved. The other boys looked up then, and I waved shyly to them. I was about to say something when I heard my mother's angry voice. "Elizabeth Ann! Get off that bed! Look, you got dirt on Daddy's pillow standing on it with your shoes on. And you know it's wrong to look at naked boys. You should be ashamed of yourself! Those boys are dirty heathens, and you are not allowed to look at them or talk to them."

I can't even describe how crushed I felt. For the first time in my life, I had seen children playing happily together, and I had had a rare moment of joy. But my mother had just told me that I could not participate in similar activities. I didn't understand how or why I was different from them, but I was quite sure at that moment that I would never, ever enjoy the company of other children. As far as I could see, I was destined to live a perpetually lonely, boring life in solitary confinement.

I felt enormous grief and heavy despondency. I had just seen children playing together, and I deeply yearned for that kind of freedom and connection and enjoyment. But I believed that I would never have the opportunity to experience it. I sank into a dejected, hopeless mood, believing that my life was going to be perpetually lonely and devoid of companionship.

Solitary confinement had already been boring and unpleasant, but I had accepted it as the only life I knew. Now that I had seen other children playing happily together, suddenly my life felt extremely meager and miserable.

I could not express my sadness, and I didn't believe that my mother could understand or would even try to understand what I was unhappy about. She was solely focused on being the most perfect missionary wife she could possibly be, and that included raising perfect Christian children. I was sure that I would never be allowed to play freely and happily with other children. And now that I had seen that as a possibility, I felt enormous sorrow and emptiness. I felt completely powerless to find a way to experience that kind of joy. I felt sadder and lonelier than ever.

When Daddy came home, Mommy told him that she had seen me looking out the window at the noisy, dirty naked boys playing in the street. I just hung my head. Daddy looked at me as though he understood some of what I was feeling, but he just said, gently, "You need to obey your mother."

I could not think of any way to persuade my parents to let me play with other children, especially because the children I had seen playing together were all boys. I was already well aware that many opportunities open to males were not available to females.

I promised myself again that, when I grew up, I would remember how I felt as a child, and I would be kind to my children. Meanwhile, it seemed like growing up was taking so long—so … very … long. I wondered if I was ever, ever going to get past the age of three so that, one day, I would become an adult and be able to make my own choices.

CHAPTER 5

Learning about God

Comayaguela, Honduras, 1947

MY PARENTS HAD BOTH GROWN up in homes where daily Bible reading and prayer were taken very seriously. They continued the habit after their marriage and for the rest of their lives. So, naturally, I was introduced to the Bible at a very early age.

I'm sure I was very young when my mother told me how God created the heavens and the earth. I could look up and see the sky, with the assurance that God had made it. I could see the soil and trees and other plants that God had made. I could even picture God, a big man made out of fluffy white clouds, with a long white beard, living in the sky. I could picture God taking handfuls of clay to make different animals. Once I had made a snake out of clay—it was fun to roll the clay between my hands and watch it grow longer. I imagined that God made a snake the same way.

I heard the story of God creating Adam and then taking a rib out of Adam to make a "helpmeet" for him, a woman named Eve. I heard that they lived in the beautiful garden of Eden. God told them they could eat whatever they wanted but not the fruit of one tree in the middle of the garden. But a snake told Eve to eat it, and Eve told Adam to eat it, so they ate the fruit they were not supposed to eat. Then God got mad at them for disobeying Him and made them leave the beautiful garden and go to a place that was not nearly so nice.

At this point, I asked my mother, "Mommy, why did Adam and Eve have to leave the garden of Eden?"

"Because they disobeyed God. We are supposed to obey God and do what He tells us to do."

"But why couldn't they stay in the garden?"

"That was God's way of punishing them for being bad."

"Does God punish children too?

"God gave you parents to take care of you, and through the Bible, God teaches us what to do."

"Will you make me leave the house if I disobey you?"

"Of course not!"

"Then why was God so mean to Adam and Eve? I don't like God!"

"You must never say that. We are supposed to love God."

I was beginning to learn, at a very young age, that I could have my own opinions, but it was usually safer not to say them out loud.

Another story she read to me was about Noah and his ark. I was fascinated by the story of all the animals going in two by two—elephants and zebras and giraffes and monkeys! But I was horrified at the idea that the flood had been sent by God to destroy all the people who were so wicked.

"Mommy, why did God send a flood?" I asked.

"It was because the people were so wicked that God had to destroy them."

"Were all the people wicked, even the little children?"

"I guess so."

"Even the babies?"

"I don't know. I need to go make supper now. Why don't you go play with your dolls?"

So I went and spanked my dolls, because they were bad.

I wondered what God would do if there were lots and lots of bad people today. Maybe I was even one of the bad people. I knew I wasn't really a good person because I didn't always obey my parents. I tried to please my parents, but no matter how hard I tried to be good they never seemed happy with me. And I didn't know how to please God. I couldn't understand what God wanted from me. And besides that, I didn't like God.

But I was afraid of what God would do to me, so I tried to be good. Still, I didn't think God liked me either.

I knew that the story of Noah and the ark was true, because the Bible said that God put a rainbow in the sky when He promised not to send another flood like that one, and I had actually seen a rainbow.

I liked to see rainbows, and I liked to think that God would not send another flood like that. But I suspected that God could think of other ways to punish and kill bad people. And almost everyone was bad. I wondered how bad people had to be before God punished and killed them.

I had been told that God is great, and God is good. I was also told that the Bible is the Word of God. How could they both be true? The God of the Bible, rather than seeming to be great and good often came across to me as mean and scary and unpredictable. Because I was subjected to Bible reading every day, I accepted the idea that the Bible was the Word of God. But to me, it negated the idea that God was great or good. Thus, I listened to Bible reading every day while believing that the God of the Bible was unlovable and fear provoking. At a very young age, I was picturing God as a creator and also a cranky old man who was very hard to please and who had a propensity toward harsh punishments. I was very afraid of God, and I fully expected Him to give me some kind of horrible punishment, maybe when I least expected it.

CHAPTER 6

Other Stories

Comayaguela, Honduras, 1947

SOMETIMES MY MOTHER READS ME stories that are not in the Bible. I like to listen to those stories because they are more fun, and I don't have to believe them unless I want to. As I listen to my mother read The Tale of Peter Rabbit, I like to pretend that I am Peter Rabbit, and I also pretend that I am Flopsy and Mopsy and Cottontail. Flopsy and Mopsy and Cottontail are good little girl rabbits. I usually try to be a good little girl, but I wish I could be a brave little boy like Peter, even if he gets in trouble.

As soon as his mother leaves, Peter goes straight into Mr. McGregor's garden, just after being told not to go there. How was he brave enough to be so bad? Did he think he really wasn't going to get in trouble? How did Peter know what to eat?

My heart beats fast when Peter sees Mr. McGregor by the end of the cucumber frame, planting out young cabbages. I hold my breath when Mr. McGregor is chasing Peter, and I feel happy when Peter finds a hiding place in a watering can. Finally, he discovers a way out of the garden and runs out, leaving his jacket and shoes behind.

I know rabbits don't really wear clothes or speak English, but I like it that they wear clothes and speak English in the story. It makes them seem more like me, and at the same time, it makes everyone know that they are not really real. I like stories that are made up just for fun, and I like not having to believe them—not like Bible stories. They might sound like stories, but because they're in the Bible, we're supposed to believe them and remember them.

When Peter comes home, without his clothes and not feeling well, his mother takes care of him even though he disobeyed her. Old Mrs. Rabbit is nicer than God because she still lets Peter live at home, not Like God when he made Adam and Eve leave the garden of Eden, the only home they ever knew. He didn't give them a second chance.

I think God is not fair and certainly not nice. I wish there was the kind of God I could love, but the only God I know about is mean and scary. There must be something wrong with me that I can't love God the way I'm supposed to. And I'm also quite sure that God does not like me very much, either.

I try not to think about God. I play with my dolls, and I tell them nice stories, and I don't tell them about God.

CHAPTER 7

A New Baby

Comayaguela, Honduras, 1947

I DIDN'T KNOW THAT MY PARENTS had secretly been working to produce a younger sibling for me. I do not remember being told anything about the impending arrival of a new member of the family. When I was three and a half, early in the morning of November 25, 1947, I woke up and called for Mommy.

Instead of Mommy, Daddy came. He picked me up and carried me into Mommy and Daddy's bedroom. There was light from a kerosene lamp on a table, and lying in bed beside Mommy was a little pink baby. It looked sort of like one of my dolls, but it was wrinkly, and it didn't have much hair and no teeth. Daddy said, "This is your new baby sister, Ruth Mary."

Mommy and Daddy looked very proud and happy. I did not feel happy at all. How did this baby get here? My life was already bad enough; it would probably get worse with a stupid baby in the house. There was nothing I could do about it; Baby Ruth was here to stay.

Incidentally, the physician who assisted in the home birth of Ruth was Dr. Ramon Villeda Morales, who became the president of Honduras a few years later.

Baby Ruth cried a lot. I made up a little song that I sang quietly to myself:

O cry, Baby Ruth,
O cry, Baby Ruth,
O cry Baby Ruth,
O cry.

Once when I was wearing a dress that buttoned down the front, I saw Mommy sitting on a wicker chair with Baby Ruth sucking milk from one of her nipples. I unbuttoned my dress and started feeding my doll with my little nipple.

Mommy said, "Oh, are you feeding your doll?" in such an embarrassing voice that I buttoned up my dress and didn't feed my doll anymore.

Taking care of Baby Ruth took a lot of Mommy's time and attention—feeding her, changing her diapers, rocking her to sleep, and tending to her when she cried, which was very often. Mommy had even less time to read me the stories I liked to hear, and she often seemed tired and short-tempered. I tried to entertain myself, but I still had trouble finding things to do.

Eventually Will came home from boarding school, and that helped a little. Sometimes he would play with me, and there was someone besides the stupid baby for me to be with.

When Baby Ruth started to crawl and then walk and talk, she was challenging in new ways. She had a lot of energy, and she learned to move very fast, so we had to watch her so she wouldn't hurt herself. Sometimes I was supposed to watch her, but I wasn't too good at doing that. And when she started talking, her favorite word was, "No!" She often did things that our parents told her not to do, and even if they spanked her, she kept on doing them. It was hard for me to understand. I didn't like to be spanked, and I didn't like for my parents to be angry or annoyed with me. Maybe she didn't like being punished, but it didn't stop her from doing what she wanted to do. Sometimes I could play with her, but she usually did not want to play the way I wanted to play. Life at home was getting more complicated. Maybe it was a little less boring, but it was still not to my satisfaction.

Ruth and me with Dad on a mule

CHAPTER 8

How a Pair of Overalls Made Me a Skeptic

Princeton, New Jersey, 1949

I SPENT THE FIRST YEARS OF my childhood very restricted in my movements because I was dressed in short little dresses, and I was reprimanded whenever my panties were visible to my parents. My brother Will, who was four years older, wore short pants or long pants that completely covered his underwear, and he could run, jump, climb, and even turn somersaults without ever having to worry about being reprimanded for exposing his underwear. When I asked my mother why I had to wear a dress while Will could wear pants, Mom told me, "That's just the way it is." When people had come to our missionary home in Honduras, I noticed that all the women wore dresses, and all the men wore pants. And on the rare occasion when I saw another child, the girls always wore dresses. It was the 1940s, and that was how people dressed.

I saw that that was the way it was, but I wondered why it was that way. Maybe things could be a different way. Who had decided that girls had to wear dresses? I had a sneaking suspicion that it was God who decreed that girls had to wear dresses. That seemed to be in character with the God I believed in. He had shown Himself to be cruel and sadistic and unreasonable—punishing Adam and Eve the very first time they disobeyed Him, sending a flood to kill all the little children along with their wicked parents, and threatening to punish anyone who did not love Him. I suspected that making up a rule that women and girls had to wear dresses was one of the many ways that God worked to make people's lives (especially mine!) difficult and uncomfortable.

When I asked questions about Bible stories, I was also told, "That's just the way it is" (or was).

"Why did God create Adam and then make Eve out of Adam's rib?"

"That's just the way it was."

"Why did God send a flood to destroy all the people except Noah's family?"

"That's just the way it was."

"Did children get drownded in the flood?"

"I suppose they did."

"Is that because they were bad?"

"I don't know."

"Why did God make children get drownded in the flood?"

"God always knows best; we must not question the will of God."

I glumly accepted those answers, as I didn't know how to argue with them. I also waited impatiently for the very far-off day when I would be grown up and able to make up my own rules for myself. I would be able to go to bed and get up when I wanted. I would be able to eat what I wanted. I would be able to wear whatever I felt like wearing. And maybe I would be able to find better explanations for things than "that's just the way it is." Best of all, I would be able to get away from the disapproving eyes of my parents.

Something shifted for me when I was five. It was 1949, and we were living in New Jersey while my father studied at Princeton Theological Seminary. One morning I went into the kitchen and saw my two-year-old sister Ruth wearing overalls—overalls! On a little girl! I was insanely jealous. If I could have started wearing overalls when I was two years old, my early childhood would have been ever so much more active and free and fun. How come Ruth, who already got so much attention and good things, how come she got to wear overalls, which I never got to wear, but which would have made my life so much better? It wasn't fair!

After I got past the first blind rage of jealousy, I was able to start reasoning. If my little sister could wear overalls, then it wasn't really true that all little girls had to wear dresses. And if that wasn't absolutely true, then maybe there were other "facts" that had been presented to me that also were not absolutely true. This increased my trust in my own ability to question and to think for myself, rather than automatically accept whatever I was told.

CHAPTER 9

A Beautiful Baby

Princeton, New Jersey, 1949

IN PRINCETON, WE LIVED IN a modest apartment in a building with other missionary families of students studying at Princeton Theological Seminary. At last I had other children to play with! My favorite game to play with them was "doctor," in which we would undress and examine each other. I had previously done that with my dolls, but doing it with other children was much more satisfying. I also went to morning kindergarten, where Miss Mary Wilcox told us stories and sang songs with us and coached us through a variety of socializing activities. Kindergarteners did not learn to read in those days.

I was five and a half when my youngest sister, Eunice, was born. Unlike the home birth of my sister Ruth, three years earlier, Eunice was born in a hospital. Dad was in the midst of final exams at the seminary, so he arranged for neighbors to help out with us children at home. Mom and Baby Eunice were kept in the hospital for about a week. Unlike today's new mothers, Mom was kept on strict bed rest for several days and allowed only very gentle excursions at first. Dad went to see Mom and the new baby every day, but children were not allowed. After each visit, Dad told us that Eunice was a beautiful baby. "Even the nurses say that she is one of the most beautiful babies they have ever seen," he would add.

I had several days to anticipate the new baby's arrival at home. During that time, I created a mental picture of my beautiful baby sister. She would look like the most beautiful baby doll I had ever seen—curly hair, smooth skin with rosy cheeks, and little baby teeth. I had this picture firmly in my mind when Baby Eunice finally arrived home. Mom entered carrying a well-wrapped bundle to shield her from the December cold, and several other adults followed her into our small apartment. The new baby was laid out on a bed and unwrapped. I managed to squeeze through the crowd of adults standing around admiring her.

What I saw gave me another reason not to trust adult judgment. Instead of a lovely china doll, my new baby sister was red and wrinkled, hairless, and toothless. I already knew that adults' opinions were often not trustworthy. This was just another example. These grown-ups had no idea of real beauty! Once again, I decided it was better to trust my own opinions rather than those of the adult authority figures around me. I was learning to rely on myself for my own truth in matters of personal beliefs and behavior—and now in matters of aesthetics as well.

CHAPTER 10

First Grade

Sutter, Illinois, 1950

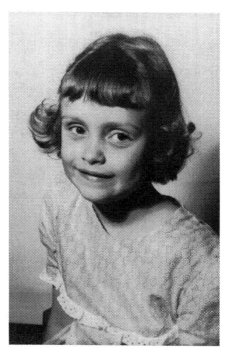

My first grade picture

WHEN I WAS SIX, WE traveled to Illinois. Since my father had been away from his extended family for a long time, going to Illinois required a visit to all the relatives. Visiting relatives. I dreaded those words. My dad would drive up the road, with gravel crunching under the tires of our 1947 black Pontiac, us three older children in the back seat, and Mom holding baby Eunice in the front seat. Dad would give a couple of excited beeps on the car horn. A woman in a housedress and apron would bustle out of the front door onto the porch, and a man in overalls would appear from the barnyard.

Whether we were visiting Uncle Frank and Aunt Hilda, Uncle Ed and Aunt Bertha, or Aunt Sophie and Uncle Frank, the routine was the same. The aunt and uncle would greet us, and to me they would say, "My how you've grown!" always, predictably, the same expression. Then the grown-ups would sit in the living room for hours, talking about things that were not the least bit interesting to me, and I was supposed to be quiet and stay out of the way. B-o-r-i-n-g. There were seldom other children to play with, as most of my aunts and uncles' children were much older.

At Uncle Sam and Aunt Hester's house, it was different. Uncle Sam was Dad's oldest brother, a short, wiry man with weathered skin from decades of farming. His wife, Aunt Hester, was of average height and much greater than average weight. She loved to cook, and she loved to eat. She had a hearty laugh, and to me she was the ideal "jolly fat person." They lived in an old farmhouse that had lots of drawers in the kitchen. Aunt Hester would invite me into the kitchen and show me the drawer where she kept puzzles. I loved putting puzzles together, and I appreciated Aunt Hester's kind attention. She also gave me cookies, including crunchy vanilla cream wafers that tasted sort of like ice cream cones. And sometimes when I had finished with the puzzles, she would notice that I was getting bored and find something more for me to do. I am still grateful to Aunt Hester for noticing me and treating me with such kindness.

We moved into the upstairs apartment of Uncle Ed and Aunt Bertha's farmhouse. Sometimes I would creep timidly down the stairs only to find Uncle Ed ready to tease me by pretending to sweep me with a broom. I would quickly run back upstairs crying, "Mommy, Uncle Ed! Uncle Ed!"

Uncle Ed loved to tease us, and he also enjoyed finding ways to amaze his nephew and nieces, such as taking his hands off the steering wheel when he was driving (in my childish ignorance, I thought the steering wheel was what made the car go) or playing a tape recording (new technology at the time) of his baby grandson laughing. But I was shy and unaccustomed to being teased, so I would run away when Uncle Ed started teasing me.

Uncle Ed and Aunt Bertha had one daughter, Arlene, but she was grown up and married and lived far enough away that we seldom saw her and her small son. There were no other children close to Uncle Ed's farm.

Grandma Limkemann was staying in a bedroom downstairs. She was always lying in a big bed, and sometimes I would sit on a little stool beside her bed and play with my dolls. Periodically she would ask me to bring her bottle of medicine. I would do that, and she would take her medicine. Then, after I replaced the bottle on the dresser, she would ask me to bring her the paper sack from the dresser. When I did that, she would take a piece of candy out of the sack and give it to me. I'm happy to have a few pleasant memories of her, as a few months later, I saw her body lying in a coffin in Uncle Ed and Aunt Bertha's living room.

Summer on the farm included rolling in the grass, smelling newly mown hay, feeding chickens in the chicken yard (they would come around and peck at my legs), and seeing the little piglets with their mother in the pigpen.

My time at Uncle Ed's farm was not particularly happy, as illustrated by this incident. I was outside alone near the house one day when I noticed the machinery that was part of the windmill that pumped water from the well. Out of curiosity I touched the belt that connected the windmill to the pump, and my hand got caught in it. I screamed and cried with pain and fear, and even though Mom and Aunt Bertha were nearby in the house, with open windows, nobody came to my rescue until I continued to scream and cry for a long time. They were so accustomed to hearing my cries of anger and frustration that it didn't occur to them at first that I might have a "real" reason to cry. Fortunately, the belt was loose, and my hand recovered quickly.

My prevailing mood changed suddenly the day before I started first grade. I had received my first grade reader, a colorful book about Dick and Jane and Sally and their dog, Spot, and their cat, Puff. My ten-year-old cousin, Delbert, was visiting that day. Sitting on the porch of Uncle Ed's house, Delbert pointed to the words in my reader and carefully pronounced each word. I had learned the alphabet, but I had not yet started to read. As he pointed to each word with his finger and read it out loud, I suddenly understood how letters were organized into words! The pictures in the book also helped me to understand what the words were and what they meant. I could read! Within just a few minutes, I had gone from not knowing how to read to being someone who could read! I was ecstatic!

One-room schoolhouse

The next day, I walked to the one-room country schoolhouse with my brother, Will, and some other children. I tried to keep up with them, but my short legs had a hard time going as fast as the older children, and soon I had a stitch in my side and had to stop and rest. I felt the impatience of the other children, but I didn't know what else to do.

The schoolhouse was a small wooden building, painted white, at the end of a gravel road. There were three steps leading up to a narrow porch and the door to the school. Straight ahead inside the door was the teacher's large wooden desk and chair, with a blackboard on the wall behind it. There were six chairs in a semicircle beside her desk. First graders sat at small desks in the front of the classroom, and there was a progression of age and size toward the back of the room. There were windows on both sides and a wood-burning stove near the middle of the wall opposite the door. With only a few children in each grade (grades one through eight), the teacher kept very busy teaching lessons and giving assignments to each group. I liked watching and listening to the lessons of the older students after I'd finished my assignment. Our teacher fostered a cooperative attitude in the classroom and sometimes asked one of the older students to work with some of the younger students.

Behind the school there were two wooden outhouses with the characteristic crescent moon cutouts in the door. One was for boys, the other for girls. Inside each outhouse there was a wooden ledge with a hole cut out so that body waste products would drop into the pit beneath. I didn't dare look into it, and I didn't like the smell in there, but I used it when I had to. Usually there were flies buzzing around. For toilet paper, there was an old Sears and Roebuck catalogue hanging on a wire suspended from a nail in the wall.

In front of the school was an iron pump handle with a water dipper attached with a chain. Whenever someone needed water for drinking or hand washing, they would pump the handle up and down, and it would creak with a rusty singsong voice, eventually bringing water up from the well. Everyone drank from the one metal dipper attached to the pump.

I loved going to school. I loved having new experiences and mastering new skills. I liked being with other children of various ages. And I especially appreciated being in a situation where I understood the rules and knew how to follow them. At home, I often did not know what action or attitude was going to provoke disapproval from my parents. Letting my panties show, talking too loudly, opening my eyes during family prayers, being unwilling to go to bed, leaving dolls lying around naked—all were likely to earn a reprimand or even a spanking.

Once I thought I was being really good by very quietly sewing together a dress for my doll while my parents were taking their Sunday afternoon nap. When Mommy finally got up, I proudly showed her the red-and-white checked dress I had sewed with crude stitches of strong black thread. She scolded me for "working on the Sabbath." I was crushed. I had no idea that making a doll dress on Sunday was forbidden. I just couldn't please her not matter how hard I tried.

But at school, if I paid attention and did what I was told, the teacher praised me for it. Because I was already able to read, she was soon giving me more advanced work to do.

About the same time that I started first grade, I also started piano lessons. I practiced on the old upright piano in Uncle Ed and Aunt Bertha's living room, and I enjoyed playing simple songs on the piano and learning to read music. Previously I had tinkered with the piano keyboard, and I had learned one simple tune: "Peter Peter Pumpkin Eater." Now I was learning to play tunes that I could sing, and I was learning to read music. I was thrilled! In addition, I was getting approval from my parents for my willingness to practice the piano. Sometimes my father even sang along with my simple songs.

After two months in the Illinois schoolhouse, I was enrolled in a similar schoolhouse in rural Missouri, where we had gone to stay with my Grandma and Grandpa Peters while Dad went to the Panama Canal Zone to start his new job and prepare for our move there. My new school had only six grades in one room, and I had several other first graders to learn with and play with. I also enjoyed going to that school.

In January 1951, we boarded a United Fruit Company ship on its way to Panama to pick up a load of bananas. We were the only passengers on the freighter, and after an uneventful trip, we moved into our new apartment above my father's office in the Panama Canal Zone.

I was put on a school bus and delivered to a two-story brick building with a dozen separate classrooms and a principal's office. In my classroom, there were twenty-five children, all first graders sitting at little desks and being taught first-grade curriculum by Miss Jones. I was not happy in that situation. When I got bored with my first-grade work, which happened frequently, there were no other grades being taught in my classroom, so I had to endure boredom.

In my previous school, I had learned cursive writing, but Miss Jones insisted that all first graders must print. I had to learn how to print all over again. The teacher did not like the way I made a capital C, which I made as a half-circle. She showed me how the ends of the half-circle needed to extend vertically. Oh, it's like the C on a Cheerios box, I thought.

Another adventure in relearning printing was writing a report after a class activity. There was a boy called Buddy in my class, but when I wrote about him, I pointed the ds the wrong way, so his name came out as Bubby. The other children in my class thought that was funny, and so did I.

Eventually, first grade ended, and I had a few months at home before starting second grade. I did not last long in second grade. If I had been bored in my first grade classroom, I was even more bored when Mrs. Sink carefully reviewed first-grade concepts for those who had forgotten or never understood them in the first place. I was more than ready to learn new things, but all I got was the same old lessons from first grade.

I complained loudly enough that my parents did something about it. I was put in a room by myself to complete a standardized test, which measured my knowledge and comprehension. And soon I found myself in Miss Kern's third grade class. Within a few weeks, I had caught up with them and was once again enjoying learning.

CHAPTER 11

The Panama Canal Zone

IN 1949, WHILE MY FATHER was studying at Princeton Theological Seminary in Princeton, New Jersey, he was approached by Dr. Raymond Gregory, who was employed by the American Bible Society in Central America. Dr. Gregory was getting ready to retire, and he was eager for my father, Jacob Limkemann, to fill his position. After being interviewed by some of the top executives of the American Bible Society, he was offered the position in August 1950. He went to Panama that September, and in January 1951, he returned to the United States to travel with the family from Missouri, where we had been staying with my mother's parents, to New Orleans. There we boarded a ship to go to Panama.

The Panama Canal Zone was a strip of land about ten miles wide, with the canal in the middle, stretching fifty miles from the Atlantic Ocean to the Pacific Ocean. It effectively separated the northern part of Panama from the southern part of Panama.

In the 1950s, the Panama Canal Zone was a tropical paradise, carefully maintained for the white, middle-class Americans who worked there. There were people who were directly involved with the functions of the canal—those who maintained the locks, made necessary inspections, kept the operations running smoothly, and helped to guide ships through the locks. In addition to those people and their families, there was a whole supporting community of teachers, doctors, policemen, and so on—all well paid and living in houses built and maintained by the Panama Canal Company. There were additional, separate towns for black workers and their families, most of them from Jamaica. They had their own separate community and their own schools, and they were paid much less than the white workers.

Although my family was not connected in any way to the Panama Canal Company, we lived in the Panama Canal Zone and were given special privileges to attend Canal Zone schools and to use the facilities maintained for Canal Zone families.

In the 1950s, there were a few radio stations, but television had not yet arrived in that part of the world. There were no computers and no calculators. People used slide rules for advanced math problems. There were no cell phones, of course, and no answering machines. Our phone number was only five digits. (My grandmother in Iowa had a four-digit phone number, and calling long distance was complicated and expensive, requiring the aid of a telephone operator.) We had one phone connected to the wall by a cord. Area codes and zip codes had not been invented.

We lived in Old Cristobal, on the Atlantic side of the Isthmus of Panama. (An isthmus is a narrow strip of land with water on both sides and connecting two larger bodies of land. We always enjoyed talking about "Christmas on the isthmus.") From our apartment, we could see ships about to enter the canal and ships that had just completed the trip through the canal. There was a large docking area two blocks from our house where cargo was loaded and unloaded and where passengers boarded ships. I often heard the chattering of men crowding the streets on their way to work at the docks.

Also near our home was a well-built brick post office with a small library upstairs for the use of Canal Zonians and a police station with a small jail cell directly across the street from our building.

Nearby was a recreational building, which included a cafeteria, a barbershop, a movie theater, and a small convenience store. It was there that I bought Life Savers and chewing gum with an occasional nickel or dime, gradually progressing to Milky Way candy bars and candy cigarettes and comic books and then to hairspray and my first clandestine issue of True Confessions, a pulp magazine with vaguely racy stories that appealed to my adolescent curiosity. I also saw a number of movies there, coming out of the badly air-conditioned theater reeking of cigarette smoke. People routinely smoked in theaters at that time.

My father often went on Saturdays to "have his ears lowered" at the barbershop. And on very rare occasions, our whole family would eat a meal in the cafeteria.

CHAPTER 12

Music in Our Family

IN OUR FAMILY, SINGING WAS almost as common as talking. We sang grace before meals, such as "Praise God, from whom all blessings flow." We sang children's play songs such as "London Bridge Is Falling Down." We sang songs we learned in school. Mom sang to Baby Eunice as she was putting her to bed. We sang hymns, sometimes all together, and sometimes Mom or Dad sang hymns by themselves.

Mom enjoyed the Protestant hymn called "Bringing in the Sheaves." When she was taking freshly laundered sheets off the clothesline, she sometimes changed the words to "bringing in the sheets."

Sometimes at meals, one child would start singing. Because it interfered with conversation, my parents made a rule that we all enforced: "No singing at the table." I later used the same rule with my children.

Mom played the piano reasonably well, and she often played the piano for family hymn singing. When I became proficient enough, she would often ask me to play the piano for family hymn singing, which happened at least once a week.

Maybe because we had so much music in the home—almost all live music, hardly ever recorded music—all my life I have had tunes in my head, often erupting in singing or humming or whistling. Sometimes it's an annoying tune that plays over and over in my mind, but most often, it's music that I enjoy, such as a theme from a Mozart piano sonata or a Beethoven symphony or hymns from church or popular songs from my youth or a piece one of my students is currently learning.

Because of this emphasis on music, it is not surprising that all of us children had music lessons. Soon after we arrived in the Canal Zone, I was taken to the home of Mrs. Genis, who would be my piano teacher for many years. She was a serious musician who had studied music at Drake University in Iowa and was also our church organist. Over the years that I studied with her, she guided me through the whole John Thompson piano course, from Teaching Little Fingers to Play through grade five. The motto on the cover of the John Thompson books was "something new every lesson," and Mrs. Genis did a good job of presenting new material. She wrote my assignment each week in a small brown notebook, and she expected me to practice diligently. She would scold me if I did not do as well as she expected, so I tried to learn as well as I could. My parents also insisted on daily piano practice, often setting a timer for the minimum length of required practice.

My sisters also started piano lessons with Mrs. Genis by the time they were six or seven years old. Meanwhile, Will was learning to play the violin, which he played in the junior high and high school orchestra, and he eventually also played the tuba in the band.

For several years, my father had a secretary, who was also a pianist, in his office, which was directly below our second-floor apartment. More than once when I was practicing the piano, she called on the telephone to tell me that I was forgetting the B flat or some such thing. I would look at the book I was using and see that there was, indeed, a B flat that I had overlooked. At first, I wondered how she knew, but eventually I became so accustomed to sounds that I could easily correct my own mistakes. I'm not sure how loud it was downstairs. But between my sisters and me, we provided plenty of music for the people in my father's office.

Week after week, Mom drove us to Mrs. Genis's house for our weekly piano lessons, and month after month my parents wrote checks to pay for our lessons. Obviously, they considered music lessons to be an essential part of their duties as parents.

Once a year, Mrs. Genis had her students play in a recital, by memory. Before my first recital, Mrs. Genis told me a little about it. She told me that her other students and their parents would be there, and afterward there would be little cakes. She asked me if I liked "little cakes." Of course I liked any kind of cake, but I had never heard of cupcakes being referred to as "little cakes."

My parents made a big deal out of my first recital. My mother made me a lovely white organdy dress trimmed with lace. I played "Berceuse" from Jocelyn by Benjamin Goddard. I had no idea that berceuse meant "cradlesong." I liked the tune, and I think I played it well enough.

Some students did not fare so well. I have heard many sad stories of individuals who became so nervous and flustered at the yearly piano recital that their bad experience led them to give up piano study, never to return. When I thought about that, years later, as a piano teacher myself, I decided that rather than one all-important piano recital once a year, I would have my students play for each other at informal recitals every month or two. This has worked very well. Students have frequent opportunities to prepare pieces to play; they become accustomed to playing in front of an audience; and, if their performance is below standard, we work to make sure that their next performance is more satisfying.

When I was a teenager, Mrs. Genis organized a music theory class for three of her most advanced students. Once a month, Emily and Ramona and I went to Mrs. Genis's house to learn about scales and chords and analysis of music. One day when none of us could come up with the answers she was looking for, Mrs. Genis suggested, in mock exasperation, that she should refund our parents the money they had paid for theory classes since we hadn't learned anything.

(Later when I was in college, my professor Dr. Richard T. Gore would exclaim in a similar vein, "I've taught you everything I know, and still you know nothing!")

Mrs. Genis played the organ at church, and I don't recall ever hearing anything that didn't sound right. She was always well prepared, even though I don't think she practiced much. In fact, I once asked her if she practiced the piano, and she said no. She lived in a neighborhood of homes fairly close together, all with windows wide open in the tropical heat, and she didn't want to subject her neighbors to more piano playing than was necessary for her teaching.

Mr. and Mrs. Genis moved away when I was about fifteen. Although I had never played the organ, I had better keyboard skills than anyone else in the church, so I was hired as the church organist. I had no teacher to help me at first, so I learned by experience. I had to learn to set a reasonable tempo for hymn singing and maintain a steady tempo throughout the hymn. I had to learn how loudly to play—tricky because the organ sounded louder in the front of the church, where I was, than it did in the back of the church. I had to find and learn suitable pieces to play for preludes and postludes. I began learning to use the pedals with my feet—hard to coordinate at first, but I gradually improved.

After learning on the job for the better part of a year, I then had an opportunity to take some organ lessons at Wheaton College when we were staying near Wheaton, Illinois, for the summer. My father had graduated from Wheaton, so he was happy that I had an opportunity to get somewhat acquainted with the campus and the general tone of the college—very conservative but also friendly.

After Mrs. Genis moved away, we had a new piano teacher, Maritza Tagaropoulos Kitras. I had known her slightly when she was in high school and I was in junior high. She had gone away to college, had gotten married, and had come back to Panama. She came to our house and taught my sisters and me, quite skillfully, and she helped me prepare for college.

I usually enjoyed playing the piano. I enjoyed the way my fingers felt on the piano keys, and I learned many wonderful and memorable pieces. However, there was a time when I was eleven or twelve years old that I told my mother I wanted to quit piano lessons. She asked me to finish the book I was working through at the time (I think it was Thompson grade four), and then, if I still wanted to quit, she would let me. Fortunately, by the time I finished that book, I was again enjoying playing the piano.

Of course I would hear my sisters practicing, and occasionally, when nobody was looking, I would go to the piano and play one of the pieces that Ruth was working on, making the same mistakes that she usually made. I got a kick out of doing that. Sometimes Mom would walk into the room and say, "Oh, I thought that was Ruth playing."

Mr. Jorstad, who taught chorus, orchestra, and band at the junior high and high school, completely relied on his student accompanists. When I was in seventh grade, he handed me a book of accompaniments and told me to learn them. I did so, dutifully, and when it was my turn to accompany the junior high chorus, he painstakingly taught me how to follow a conductor. I had some difficulty looking at the music and also watching him while I was playing, but I caught on after a while, thanks to his careful and patient teaching.

I continued accompanying the school choirs through high school. And the skills I learned in junior high have served me well for many years.

CHAPTER 13

The Executive Director

Cristobal, Canal Zone, 1951

I WAS ABOUT SEVEN WHEN I started taking swimming lessons at the YMCA. I would walk to the Y with Will, and I had to wait in the lobby until his class was finished. As I sat with my legs dangling over the edge of a hard wooden chair, wearing my bathing suit under my clothes and holding a towel wrapped around the clothes I would wear after swimming, I had plenty of opportunities to look around.

I would gaze wistfully at all the little girls going to and from dance class in the big auditorium. Their teacher, Madge Locke, was a striking presence with her bulky figure and her red-dyed hair. I didn't know anybody else who had such obvious dyed hair. She would call out orders and count and direct the girls in their dance exercises while scratchy music played on a Victrola. I knew that I would never be allowed to take dance class. Once I had persuaded my parents to take me to a variety show (for charity), which included a few dance numbers. When I heard my mother talking indignantly about "little girls in skimpy costumes showing off their bodies in front of an audience," I knew that my parents would never give me permission to go to dance class.

Swimming lessons were different. My parents believed that knowing how to swim was an important skill for their children to learn, especially because they had never become good swimmers. My mother could not swim at all, and my father had learned the hard way, by being tossed into a deep pool in a creek where he developed his laborious, inefficient style of swimming. Since we were growing up surrounded by water, and we had the opportunity for good instruction, we were dutifully sent off to swim lessons every week.

Sitting in the lobby I noticed a door labeled "Executive Director." I never saw anyone in that office on Saturday mornings when I was there. I thought the word was pronounced /eks-e-CUTE-ive/. I did not know what an eks-e-CUTE-ive director did, but I had overheard adults talking about someone being executed, so I jumped to the conclusion that the executive director was in charge of executions. Why would the YMCA have a person in an office making decisions about executions? That seemed very strange to me. Did that person decide who was going to be executed? Why were people being executed? And who was doing the actual executions? Probably not the executive director himself. I guessed that they would not be executing children, so I was probably safe for now. I also considered the possibility that executive director did not mean what I thought it meant. Nevertheless, I thought it would be a good idea to be well behaved and not attract attention to myself, just in case.

Although it seems kind of amusing now (assigning a sinister meaning to the word executive), it also demonstrates how dangerous I perceived the world to be. Not only was I hearing about many violent deeds in the Bible—the Great Flood, David killing Goliath, and Joshua and his men slaughtering thousands of Canaanites, to name only a few—there was plenty of uneasiness in the world at that time, even if I only heard bits and pieces once in a while. The horrors of WWII had ended only a few years before; capital punishment and lynchings were happening in the United States; and polio epidemics were going on, to name a few of the scary things in the world. I knew that my parents would protect me in the world as well as they could, but I also knew that they could not protect me from angry, punishing God.

CHAPTER 14

The Bible House

Cristobal, Canal Zone, 1951–1963

The Bible House

WE LIVED IN A LARGE three-story concrete building labeled "The American Bible Society." My father's suite of offices was on the first floor, where he presided over a secretary, a bookkeeper, and a handyman. He sent and received letters to various missionaries and ministers in Central America, which was his territory. He also corresponded regularly with the New York office of the American Bible Society. There were frequent shipments of Bibles, New Testaments, and various other biblical literature coming and going from his office. One room of his office suite was set up for wrapping packages, which were then taken to the nearby post office.

We had a large apartment on the second floor, above Dad's office. There were cool green tile floors throughout the whole apartment, and all the walls were painted light green, much to my mother's dismay. As it was a large square building, the interior rooms, including the kitchen, were rather dark. Darkness was especially appealing to cockroaches, ever present in that tropical climate. Sometimes at night as I lay in bed, I would hear my father stamping on cockroaches, which started running for cover whenever the kitchen light was turned on.

The three bedrooms had glass casement windows, which were always open except during storms of torrential rain and strong wind. The long rooms at the front and back of the apartment had no glass. What we called the front porch had metal louvers that could be opened and closed. The back porch had only screens on the windows. As that was the room where we ate many of our meals on a chrome and Formica table, Mom put up café curtains for privacy. I couldn't understand her need for privacy—what did it matter if anyone saw us eating? It wasn't like we were undressing or something like that. I puzzled over that for years. I now realize that having curtains at the windows made family meals much more intimate, as it effectively closed out the rest of the world from our mealtimes together.

An interesting feature of that room was an exposed water pipe, painted green like the walls and connected from the first floor to the apartment in the third floor above us. As a small child, Eunice enjoyed shimmying up the pipe, holding on with her hands and using her bare feet on the wall to propel her up toward the ceiling. There were often little dirty footprints on the wall. Our parents always told her to get down, with only slight annoyance. I couldn't help but notice that she enjoyed a great deal more freedom than I had at her age, due largely to the fact that she wore shorts or cute little sunsuits and did not have to be constantly vigilant about letting her panties show, as I had had to do at her age.

Across from that side of our apartment was a building with rooms for single men. We called it the bachelor quarters. There was parking at street level for the men's cars, and above that were two floors of single rooms. It was occupied by American men without families. Some were there temporarily, and some lived there for years. One crotchety man would yell at us out of his window if we were making too much noise playing outside. He may have had a nighttime job and had to sleep during the day. On Saturdays, a crew of Jamaican men came to the bachelor quarters to wash cars for a small fee. My father usually had our car washed so it would be clean and shiny for Sunday. He also wanted to support the men in their business.

We had one bathroom, an interior room with unmovable wooden louvers for privacy at the ventilation window beside the toilet. It included a claw-foot bathtub, a tile-lined shower stall, a toilet, and a sink. I bathed every evening in the bathtub, until I was ready to graduate to the shower. Dad would sometimes lead a group of children to the bathroom sink, calling it the Toothbrush Brigade. He also filled the sink with water for me to practice putting my face under water when that proved challenging in swimming class. With much encouragement, I eventually succeeded in being able to put my head under water, even with my eyes open.

Downstairs on the first floor was a laundry room where Mom washed mountains of dirty clothes every Monday in a wringer washer. She then hung everything out to dry on clotheslines strung on a sturdy framework of pipes in the backyard. When it was raining, clothes were hung in the long corridor leading to the back door of Dad's office. Around 1958, Mom's job was simplified by the acquisition of an automatic washer and dryer inside our apartment. She no longer had to lug heavy loads of laundry up and down stairs.

There were other apartments in the building. Across the hall from our front door was a three-room apartment, with a bathroom but no kitchen, and across from our back door was another small apartment. We often used the smaller apartment as a playroom, building houses of wooden blocks and drawing streets with chalk on the floor. There were two more full-size apartments on the third floor. One of the third-floor apartments was always occupied by renters. The other vacant apartments were used by missionaries traveling through. Some stayed only a few days, most no longer than a week or two. One couple had to wait several months for their visa before they could travel.

There was also a penthouse, which had been added and used by the US Navy during World War II. It had provided them with a view of ships coming close to the Atlantic side of the Panama Canal. When we lived there, the penthouse could not be occupied, because the only access to it was a single termite-eaten wooden stairway. However, my brother happily used it for his ham radio activities.

There was often a flurry of activity when guests were expected—Mom wanted to make sure the apartment was clean, with clean sheets on the beds and pitchers of water and bowls of tropical fruit ready for the guests. Sometimes there were children in the missionary families, and we were happy to take them to our playroom or our backyard to get acquainted. We were not responsible for their meals. Dad's predecessor, Dr. Gregory, had said, "We sleep 'em, but don't eat 'em." They were able to get their meals at the nearby cafeteria.

When there were no visitors in the guest rooms, my sisters and I, sometimes with friends, enjoyed a raucous pastime that we called "the Game." In our adaptation of hide-and-seek, we would run barefoot up and down the sets of concrete stairs and hide behind the walls, stealthily moving around. When somebody was caught, our excited screams would echo through the hallways. Our parents did not appreciate the noise, but we loved playing "the Game."

(Me with Ruth and Eunice)

CHAPTER 15

Church

Panama Canal Zone, 1951–1961

Cristobal Union Church

AS SOON AS WE MOVED to the Panama Canal Zone, Cristobal Union Church became a focal point of our family life. We lived in Old Cristobal (the name Cristobal being the Spanish equivalent of Christopher), and both the church and our school were in New Cristobal. Old Cristobal was separated from New Cristobal by the small but densely populated Panamanian city of Colon (the Spanish name of Columbus).

Preparation for church began on Saturday, if not earlier in the week. Our Sunday clothes would have been washed on Monday, but we had to be sure they were clean and unwrinkled; our Sunday shoes had to be clean and ready (they were to be worn only to church or for very special occasions, such as piano recitals); and Sunday school lessons had to be studied diligently. Family Bible reading did not qualify as Sunday school lesson study; we were expected to read the assigned scripture and write the answers in our Sunday school lesson booklets.

Mom was especially busy on Saturdays. She usually went out to buy food on Saturday morning, she tidied up the apartment (weekly cleaning had taken place on Friday), and she often baked a cake for Sunday dinner—all in addition to preparing Saturday meals and supervising four children. On Saturday evening, she would rub Pond's Cold Cream into her face and set her hair with pin curls or brush rollers so that she would have a suitable hairdo for going to the House of the Lord.

We got up early on Sunday mornings. We usually had crisp fried bacon and sunny-side up fried eggs for breakfast (our special Sunday breakfast), with pieces of white bread for dipping into the liquid yolks. While the rest of us were putting on our Sunday clothes and taking turns in the bathroom, Mom would be in the kitchen cleaning up after breakfast and putting a beef roast in the oven, calculating that it would be finished cooking when we returned from church. We children would line up beside the family car, a 1947 Pontiac, black and shiny from getting washed on Saturday. At the last minute, Mom and Dad would appear, Mom having transformed herself from kitchen wife to well-dressed family matriarch. In a beautiful print cotton dress (which she had made herself), white shoes, white purse, a string of beads around her neck, well-combed hair, and a discreet dab of lipstick, she was ready for church. Dad wore a white shirt and necktie, with his blue seersucker suit and his well-polished shoes. We three older children climbed into the back seat of our two-door car, and little Eunice sat in front between Mom and Dad. There were no seat belts or booster seats in that era.

We drove through the city of Colon, which usually looked quite sleepy on Sunday morning. The church was just past the far edge of Colon, across the street from a row of crowded small apartments. Cristobal Union Church was a two-story cement structure. The lower floor, with plain cement walls and floors, was the area for the younger children's Sunday school. We first gathered in the large meeting area, where we sang a few songs, accompanied on an old upright piano, and then dispersed to our individual classes. At the end of Sunday school, we each received a copy of Sunday Pix, a colorful four-page weekly publication that had stories from the Bible illustrated in comic book style, designed to entertain and edify churchgoing children.

After we were released from our Sunday school classes (Mom and Dad had been in the adult Sunday school class in the church sanctuary upstairs), we reunited with our family and prepared ourselves for the ordeal of sitting through a long, boring church service.

Even with the windows open, which they always were, it was hot and sticky inside the church. Sitting on the hard wooden pew, looking at the royal palms nodding slightly with a breath of tropical breeze, I was expected to sit still and be quiet.

Mrs. Genis was already playing the organ when we walked in. Soon it was time for the white-robed choir to sing, "The Lord is in his holy temple, let all the earth keep silence before Him."

Next, Rev. Havener took his place at the front of the church, said some prayers in a loud voice, and then announced the first hymn, "Holy, Holy, Holy." I took a hymnbook from the rack on the back of the pew in front of me and opened it. By the time I found the right number, people were already singing along with the organ. I wondered how the organist found the right page so quickly—eventually I realized that she had been told ahead of time what was going to be sung, and she didn't have to wait for the minister to announce it.

I sang along with the others, "Holy, Holy, Holy! Lord God almighty! Early in the morning our song shall rise to Thee; Holy, Holy, Holy! Merciful and Mighty! God in Three Persons, blessed Trinity!" I enjoyed singing, and it helped that the tune was easy to sing and the words were easy to follow.

When I was first learning to read in Illinois, Aunt Bertha had showed me how to follow the words of each verse in the hymnal. Unlike reading in a regular book, when reading the words of hymns, I had to skip down to the next line of music instead of the line of words directly below the first line.

After that hymn, Rev. Havener said some prayers in his loud voice. (I realize now that there was no sound amplification in our church, unlike most churches today.) When he said a prayer, I was supposed to bow my head and close my eyes and keep my hands clasped together.

Then there was the song we sang every Sunday; it was printed right inside the front cover of the hymnbook, so I didn't have to look up the page number. Besides, I knew the song from singing it many times before: "Glory be to the Father and to the Son and to the Holy Ghost, as it was in the beginning, is now and ever shall be. World without end, amen, amen."

I didn't understand very much of that. What was the Holy Ghost? Was it like a Halloween ghost, dressed up in a sheet as a disguise? Was the Holy Ghost scary? And was the world really without end? If the world had a beginning, might it not have an end, too? Not yet, of course, but eventually the world would end.

Standing up for that song got us in position for the responsive reading, also found in the hymnbook, where there was a sentence from the Bible for the minister to read and then a sentence from the Bible for everyone to read together, this time just speaking, not singing. The other time when we all spoke together was during the Lord's Prayer.

After church, we children would run up and down the stairs while our parents shook hands and visited with people. But this could not go on for too long, as Mom was anxious to get home and take the roast out of the oven before it burned.

I remember one amusing incident. When little Eunice was being potty trained, whenever she successfully produced something in the potty, our mother would say, "That's a good girl!" So she started to associate using the potty with being called a good girl.

One day after the church service, a well-meaning man said to her, "Were you a good girl in church?"

She said "No!" indignant that someone would think she had been relieving herself in church.

On Sunday afternoons, Mom and Dad usually took a nap, and we children were supposed to entertain ourselves quietly. I would read or play with my dolls. I had learned that sewing doll clothes on the "day of rest" was unacceptable. When Mom got up, sometimes she would read us a story or play songs on the piano.

Occasionally we would act out scenes from the Bible. One of my favorites was a scene from Acts 12. Our dramatization went like this:

Peter	Ruth
Angel	Eunice
Mary, mother of John Mark	Eunice
Rhoda	Betty
People praying	dolls

Scene 1: Prison where Peter is being kept. Peter is sleeping in prison. The angel comes and wakes him up.

ANGEL. Get up! Let's get out of here!

Peter's chains fall off, and he leaves the prison.

Scene 2. Mary's house where people have gathered to pray for Peter

MARY, praying. Dear God, please be with Peter while he is in prison. Help him to be strong and courageous!

(There is a knock on the door.)

RHODA. I'll get it. (Goes to the door, opens it, sees Peter there, and closes the door.)

RHODA, (speaking to Mary and people praying.) Peter is here!

MARY. You must be dreaming.

RHODA. He's really here! I saw him with my own eyes!

(Peter knocks again.)

MARY. Well, go and let him in!

RHODA. (Goes back to the door and opens it, and Peter comes in.)

MARY. Peter! You're here! How did you get out of prison?

PETER. An angel got me out. Thank you for praying for me. Tell everyone about the angel! Now I must leave. Have a good night.

Another Bible story that I acted out with my mother was the story of Samuel in the temple. Samuel as a child had gone to live in the temple with an old priest named Eli. One night Samuel was wakened from sleep by hearing his name called. Assuming it was Eli, he went to Eli and said, "Here I am. You called me." Eli said, "I didn't call you. Go back to sleep." Again, Samuel heard his name being called and went to Eli. Again, Eli said he had not called Samuel and told him to go back to sleep. When it happened a third time, Eli told Samuel that it was the Lord calling, and he should answer, "Speak, Lord, for your servant is listening." What impressed me most about that story was that God actually spoke to a child!

Sunday evening was another special meal. We traditionally had toasted cheese sandwiches (Velveeta cheese on white bread), along with hot cocoa and a Jell-O salad made with grated carrots.

After supper, we all got busy preparing for Monday. Mom sorted laundry and started soaking soiled items in bleach, and we children got our homework together and set out our school clothes for the next day.

CHAPTER 16

What I Learned in Sunday School

Canal Zone, 1951–1961

SUNDAY SCHOOL WAS WHERE I received instruction about the Bible that was not from my parents. When I was quite young, Sunday school usually included coloring pictures of Adam and Eve in the garden of Eden or an assortment of animals on Noah's ark, with a rainbow in the background or a picture of Jesus with children on his lap. We sometimes had craft projects, such as making crosses out of Popsicle sticks or making paper doll robes for cardboard cutouts of children who lived in the time of the Bible.

And of course there were Bible stories. Some of the simplest and most obvious stories had to do with Adam and Eve and the snake in the garden of Eden, Noah and his family building an ark and (somehow) ushering pairs of animals into it ahead of the big rain, young David knocking out the giant Goliath with a stone from his slingshot (because God was with him), Mary and Joseph and shepherds and wise men with Baby Jesus, and Jesus calling fishermen to be his disciples. We saw pictures of men and women and children wearing robes that came down past their knees. We heard stories about people who had strange singular names, with no middle names or last names.

Eventually we studied other parts of the Bible. We learned that the Israelites had been enslaved in Egypt. Pharaoh had been so reluctant to let them go that God had had to send plagues of locusts and frogs, and eventually it took the death of the firstborn in each family before Pharaoh would let them go. We learned about the Israelites wandering in the desert for forty years, eating manna that fell from the sky and drinking water that came out of the rock. I thought of manna as slightly sweet flakes that fell on the ground—sort of heavenly trail mix. That might have been fun and good tasting at first, but I would think they would have gotten tired of it after forty years.

I learned about them arriving at the Promised Land—and finding it already occupied. A few men went ahead to see what was there and returned with huge bunches of grapes and other remarkable goodies. God's plan for the Israelites to inhabit the Promised Land was for them to kill all the people who already lived there. God told them to do it, so it was right and holy. Joshua fought the battle of Jericho, and the walls came tumbling down.

I had been conditioned to accept Bible stories as being true and accurate. But over time, I had many nagging questions. Why couldn't God take them to a place that was not already occupied? Surely Almighty God could have found them a home that was unoccupied. Did God have so little love for the current inhabitants that He didn't mind having them slaughtered? Wasn't the same God the God of those people? That made me feel even more insecure, because I was absolutely convinced that God didn't care for women nearly as much as He cared for men. I felt uneasy thinking that almighty, powerful God had His special favorites, and to hell with everyone else.

I could not ask the real questions. At the time I could not even think the real questions, because I was conditioned to believe that the Bible was the Word of God, and God was all good. If God was good, how was it possible to explain the inconsistencies in the Bible? I would sometimes hear the phrase, "The ways of God are mighty and mysterious." But that did not keep me from pondering, trying to understand and trying to explain the inconsistencies and the apparently immoral thoughts and actions of "God" as portrayed in the Bible.

I felt very much alone in my questioning because it seemed that nobody else had the same questions. Didn't anyone else observe that the supposedly all-loving God sometimes behaved in very unloving ways? I expected that our Sunday school teachers were already fully indoctrinated, but I wondered why none of the other students seemed to have the kind of problems with the information that I was having.

Maybe that was because the other students were not really paying attention to the Bible stories. In Sunday school classes, I was sometimes aware of a drone of mental noise, or maybe it was the students' inattention and a desire to just get through the hour as painlessly as possible.

One of my only clear memories of Sunday school was of looking at my Sunday school teacher's mouth in fascination, watching a thin thread of saliva forming between her upper tooth and bottom lip. Whatever we were doing, we usually were not actually taking in the teachings of the Bible, or maybe we were trying not to take them in.

Even my most basic questions were often lost in the hypnotic haze of Sunday school and Bible reading. I also tried to ignore the questions that were forming in the back of my mind. I knew that both in church and at home, it was forbidden by parents, ministers, and Sunday school teachers to question the truth of the Bible and the goodness of the God described in the Bible.

Recently I asked my sister Eunice if she had questions related to all the Bible readings we were forced to listen to as children. She responded that she wasn't really paying attention. (Astonishing! She was subjected to daily Bible reading for eighteen years, just as I was, but she managed to let it wash past her without it affecting her. Similarly, I have played more than eighteen years of Catholic Masses, and I pay only enough attention to play music at the appropriate times.) My sister Ruth, on the other hand, has come to treasure the Bible. She has a very sweet and loving attitude toward the Bible, and she engages in frequent Bible study.

In some churchgoing families, Sunday school and church were the only place where family members were exposed to the Bible. In our family, daily Bible reading at home was the primary form of Bible education, and Sunday school and church served as supplements to our daily study of the Word of God.

CHAPTER 17

Testing the Faith

Cristobal Canal Zone, 1952

THERE WAS A GIRL IN my Sunday school class who wore a chain around her neck with a clear glass pendant that had a little round yellow seed inside it. I knew the significance of that little yellow seed. It was a mustard seed, of which Jesus had said, "If ye have faith as a grain of mustard seed ye shall say unto this mountain, Remove hence to yonder place; and it shall remove, and nothing shall be impossible unto you" (Matthew 17:20). I pondered over that, wondering if it was really true. It sounded so easy!

Of course, I had never seen people moving mountains, not even very holy or devout people. And why would anyone want to move a mountain anyway? Just to prove that he or she had the kind of faith that Jesus talked about? But I was intrigued by the idea of faith, which was frequently a topic of discussion in my home and church.

When I was eight years old, I wasn't interested in moving mountains; I was interested in dolls. There was a doll I wanted that had a price tag of $4.99. It was a cute little boy doll—I didn't have any boy dolls— and he had the cutest little pants and shirt and a little green felt hat that especially enthralled me. He was neatly packaged in a box with a cellophane front, and I would gaze at him wistfully when I walked by the toy section in the commissary with my mother. I already had several dolls. One doll had a cloth body and painted ceramic hands and feet and head. Her beautiful eyes would close when I laid her down to sleep, and if I rocked her from front to back, she made a crying sound through a little box in her chest. My Raggedy Ann doll had yarn hair and a soft fabric body stuffed with cotton and adorable eyelet-trimmed pantalettes. I also had a "drink and wet" doll. Made of rubber, she would drink water from a miniature baby bottle through a little hole in her mouth, and sometime later, the water would seep out a hole in her bottom. The position of the hole made it seem like diarrhea rather than urine. Once I fed her cracker crumbs to see if she would have a real bowel movement. She didn't. Not even when I gave her an enema by squirting water into the hole in her bottom. I liked undressing and dressing my dolls, and sometimes I even made new clothes for them out of fabric scraps left over from Mom's sewing.

All of my girl dolls were predictably and disappointingly blank "down there." I wished that the boy doll would have some sort of male genitals, but I had no illusions that a boy doll would be anything but blank down there as well. (This was long before the days of "anatomically correct" baby dolls). I really wanted that boy doll, but I didn't have five dollars. So I decided this would be a good test of my faith. If I could summon up enough faith, surely God had the power to put a five-dollar bill behind our house.

Of course, I didn't tell my parents or anyone else about this test of faith. I had to find out for myself. There was a space about four feet wide between our building and the one-car garage behind it. That would be the perfect place for God to leave a five-dollar bill for me! Or maybe God could arrange for someone to drop a five-dollar bill there.

I worked on my faith for several days, getting it as fervent as possible—at least as big as a mustard seed and probably bigger. I knelt beside my bed and prayed. I prayed in bed before I fell asleep. I imagined what it would feel like to have total faith in God, and I cultivated that feeling in myself. I prayed really hard for God to give me a five-dollar bill.

When I had brought my faith to the greatest perfection, I decided that I was ready to go and collect the proof of my faith. I had visualized where it would be, near where the old poinsettias were planted. I walked out of my room expectantly, full of faith. I floated down the steps on a cloud of Christian virtue. I inched my way behind the building, holding my breath with suspense, and turned my eyes toward the spot where I knew it was going to be. I knew it was going to be there. I had that much faith. After all, I had summoned up all the faith I knew how to summon.

I reached the spot I had visualized and looked around. What!? It wasn't there! How was that possible? In spite of my carefully cultivated faith, God had not answered my prayer. I wasn't even asking for very much. And I had faith! I really did have faith! But it didn't work. I probably wouldn't be able to move mountains either.

Maybe nobody had that kind of faith. Maybe it was a good thing that nobody had that kind of faith, or mountains would go crashing around here and there, and nobody would be able to keep track of them. And a mountain crashing down on people could do a lot of damage. I decided that it was probably a good thing that people didn't really have the kind of faith that Jesus talked about.

But then, what was the purpose of having faith at all? What was faith all about?

CHAPTER 18

Vacation Bible School

Cristobal Canal Zone, 1952

"AW, MOM, DO I HAVE to go to vacation Bible school? And do I have to walk with her?" grumbled twelve-year-old Will, pointing derisively at me, his eight-year-old sister.

I stuck out my tongue at him.

"Yes, you do," said our mother firmly. "You will learn some new things about the Bible. And I want you to promise to stay with Betty all the way there and all the way home."

"Okay, okay," muttered Will.

Although I also didn't really want to go, I had learned that complaining didn't help my cause and just got my parents upset, so I usually, stoically, just did what I was told.

We were being made to spend five summer mornings, two hours a day, in a little church a few blocks from our home. It was a shabby wooden building belonging to a small evangelical denomination.

I now know that the fact that they had their own small church meant that the members of that church did not agree with the philosophy of the larger Union Church (a composite of several mainstream Protestant denominations), which we normally attended. The motto of the Union Church was, "Unity in essentials, liberty in nonessentials, charity in all things." The group of people who attended that small church apparently believed that they knew the truth and that everyone else was misguided. Or at the very least, they were more comfortable in a group by themselves.

I had been in small churches before. At the little church in Sutter, Illinois, when I was six years old, Aunt Bertha had showed me how to follow the words of a hymn. That same year, we stayed for a few months in the parsonage next to the small church in Hope, Missouri, where Grandpa Peters was the minister. In both those churches, in spite of rigorous and austere beliefs, I felt a warm sense of community. I did not feel such warmth in this unfamiliar church. There were a few adults and a small group of children, and there was only one child I recognized from school.

The minister greeted us, wearing a brown suit and sweating in the tropical heat. With him were two women I had not seen before. One was quite tall and thin, with her long brown hair piled neatly on top of her head. She wore wire-rim glasses, no makeup or jewelry, and her face had a pinched expression. Her long-sleeved dress was gray cotton with a small floral pattern, and it was buttoned up to her chin. The other woman was quite plump but did not look jolly the way I usually thought of fat people. Her long mousy brown hair was pulled back severely into a bun at the back of her head, and she wore an ankle-length, long-sleeved yellow dress, also buttoned up to her double chin and sturdy black oxfords with two-inch heels. (Mom had a pair of shoes like that. I called them her "tidy shoes.") She tried to smile as the children came in, but with the crease in her forehead, the smile looked more like a grimace than a welcome.

The main room was furnished with a wooden pulpit, an upright piano, and about fifty folding chairs. During the first part of the two-hour session, I sat on a folding chair with my short legs swinging freely, looking at my feet in their white socks and scuffed brown oxfords. We sang songs and listened to stories told by the minister or one of the women. Then they served us Kool-Aid in paper cups and cookies before we separated into smaller groups. Will was in a group with older kids.

In my group, we had more Bible stories and did craft projects. One of my projects was a model of a flat-roofed house like the ones people lived in when Jesus was on earth. I made it out of paper and glue, and it had crooked stairs painstakingly glued to the outside.

On the last day of Bible school, the minister talked to us about the evils of drinking. My parents never drank alcohol, and I had never been in a home were anyone was drinking. However, a few times, walking with my family in Colon, we had gone past a bar. Colon was the Panamanian city next to the Canal Zone town of Cristobal where we lived. As my parents tried to hurry us past the swinging louvered doors (like they have on saloons in western movies) I could see men sitting at small tables, and I could hear lively and rather frenetic music that made me feel momentarily frazzled. I could also smell the yeasty smell of beer. Sometimes I would see a man lurch crookedly out through the swinging doors. I wondered what kind of people went to bars and what attracted them.

As he talked about drinking, I noticed that the minister had a handsome head of brown hair and big teeth that somehow reminded me of the white keys on an accordion. He said, "You children must remember that you should never, ever drink. When people drink beer or other alcoholic beverages, they do things that they would not normally do. Sometimes they don't even know what they're doing. And they throw up. They throw up on the floor, and they throw up on themselves, and the throw up gets all over their clothes. And oh, I don't even like to talk about it," he ended distastefully. It still seems odd to me that he was talking about the evils of drinking to school-age children.

Every day at that vacation Bible school, we sang a song with the words:

> One on the outside, another on the inside,
> I'm on the inside. On which side are you?

During the song, we made gestures to point out others on the outside and myself on the inside. The simple melody reminded me of taunting tunes that we children would use to provoke each other. I wondered about the words of that song. What was the outside and what was the inside? What was so great about being inside? If being on the "inside" was such a wonderful thing, why were there so few children at this vacation Bible school (compared to several hundred children at school)? Was this small wooden church really the place where I could learn the truth about salvation? Was that why my parents had sent my brother and me there? (My sisters were still too young.)

I had many questions, and I continued to have many questions. My parents did not give satisfactory answers to most of my questions, so I learned not to reveal my questions to them, but that did not stop me from wondering—and wondering—and wondering.

CHAPTER 19

Unanswered Questions

Cristobal, Canal Zone, 1953–1955

ON A RAINY SATURDAY WHEN I was nine, I was playing with my sisters on the sofa in our living room. Ruth, age six, said, "I'll be Mrs. Havener. I have a fat stomach."

Eunice, age four, said, "You have a baby in your stomach."

I said, "If you eat lots of butter, you'll get fat quicker."

Eunice brought some pretend butter, Ruth pretended to eat it, and soon she was ready to go to the hospital (on the piano bench) so the doctor could cut open her stomach and take out the baby.

At the time we thought that a baby somehow just grew spontaneously inside the mother. A few years later, I overheard this conversation:

Six-year-old Eunice: "Dad is not my real father."

Mom: "Oh, yes he is."

Eunice: "But he didn't have anything to do with it."

Mom: "Dad is your real father." (End of conversation.)

At age eleven, I knew about the father's role. But if Mom wasn't going to tell Eunice, I certainly wasn't going to do it.

I had spent most of my first ten years being very curious about reproduction and about those interesting parts down there. I had also learned early in life that my parents did not want to answer those questions and would tell me that nice girls didn't think about such things.

My curiosity led me to books, but I was not able to find the answers I wanted. However, reading had its own pleasures, and I developed a lifelong love of books. Eventually I learned that there were books in the library containing some of the information I wanted, but they were kept on a special shelf behind the librarian's desk. Children had to have parents' permission to look at them. That didn't help me at all.

I also had questions about religion: Why do my parents read the Bible to us every day? Why do we have to believe in God? Why doesn't everyone believe in Jesus? Why is God invisible? Does God really punish people who do bad things? I was never satisfied with my parents' answers.

Sunday school classes also did not answer my real questions. I had learned early on that I must not ask troubling questions—questions that cast doubt on the Bible or the teachings of the church. Questions were okay as long as they stayed within the prescribed boundaries. Otherwise, I would cause problems and embarrass the teacher. And of course she or he would be sure to tell my parents what I had done. So I kept my real questions to myself while my classmates and I sat around a table and our teacher droned on about miracles performed by Jesus or kings of ancient Israel or some other approved information that did not seem to relate to my daily life.

This left me with only myself to puzzle over my questions. Around my parents, I tried to keep them hidden. I pretended to be clean-minded, and I tried not to exhibit resistance to daily Bible reading and prayers. I put on a show of cooperativeness to avoid getting spanked or having my mouth washed out with Ivory soap, unlike my spunky sister Ruth, whose defiant behavior often brought her such treatment.

Because my mind was a swirl of unfulfilled curiosity, questions and fears about religion, and dreaming of the day when I would finally be free of my parents' restrictions, I was not fully present most of the time. This was especially evident when playing kickball at school. Being lost in thought I wouldn't notice the ball coming toward me until it was too late. Naturally, I was usually the last child to be chosen for a team.

By way of contrast, in today's world there are plenty of opportunities to get information about sex. But it is still nearly impossible to get clear, unbiased answers to my most basic questions about religion and spirituality. Why are there so many different religions? Is the Bible really the Word of God? How did the Bible come to be so important? And how are people supposed to use the Bible?

CHAPTER 20

My Child's Eye View of Heaven

Cristobal, Canal Zone, around 1952

HEAVEN WAS PRESENTED AS THE ultimate goal for Christians. If we believed in God and in His beloved Son Jesus Christ, we would have the reward of going to heaven when we died. And death was inevitable, sooner or later.

Because I had formed my image of heaven when I was very young, I always saw myself as a young child when I thought of being in heaven. I could see myself sitting in heaven amid throngs of righteous people who had died. Heaven was kind of like a Sunday school picnic. I liked Sunday school picnics.

Once a year, the minister would announce that there was going to be a Sunday school picnic on a Saturday. The mothers would prepare special tasty food, and we would all meet at the large field by the high school. Almost everyone from the church would be there, young and old, and we looked forward to having fun together.

First came the games. In the potato sack race, the racers had their feet in a potato sack that they held up with their hands as they hopped and jumped to the finish line. The three-legged race was fun, too—whether I was running in it or just watching. Each team of two people had their ankles tied together, and they ran together toward the goal. People on the sidelines laughed and cheered. There were other games, some with balloons, and all was festive and fun.

Then it was time to eat. The bowls and platters of food were arranged on tables, and each family had plates and silverware to use. After the minister prayed a long loud prayer thanking God for our food and fellowship, we got in line to put food on our plates. I enjoyed going through the line and helping myself to the foods I liked best. Then we sat on the ground and ate. Afterward, the children ran around while the adults talked to each other. Everyone had a good time, and we left with happy memories at the end of the day.

Being in heaven would be sort of like a Sunday school picnic. There would be a lot of people of all ages sitting around. Instead of sitting on blankets on the ground, they would be sitting on clouds. It would look a lot like pictures I had seen of Jesus feeding a crowd of five thousand. Most of the people around me would be my parents and grandparents and aunts and uncles. I expected that they would continue to criticize me or ignore me, as they had in our life on earth, so the prospect of being with them in heaven did not thrill me. Mrs. Etheridge, a missionary friend of my parents who constantly corrected my grammar, would also be there.

Unlike the Sunday school picnic, there would be no food. People in heaven don't need to eat. Food is for the body we have in our life on earth. There also would be no games. We would sit there. And sit there. And sit there. Without even taking a break to go to the bathroom, because people in heaven don't need to go to the bathroom. (Although sometimes when it was raining, my brother and sisters and I would naughtily say that God was peeing. And when we heard thunder, we said that God was moving His furniture up there.) So we would sit there—for eternity. I had a sense of what eternity was like from waiting for my mother to finish talking to someone or from waiting for Christmas. But eternity in heaven just went on and on and on.

The worst part, though, the very worst part, was that we would be sitting in front of Big Bad God, who would be sitting on His huge golden throne watching us all the time. Sitting at His right hand would be Jesus on his junior throne. People would be telling God how much they loved Him and how they adored Him. I would keep quiet and hope that God didn't notice that I didn't love Him or even like Him. I didn't like the Bible, which was supposed to be the Word of God. If God was so powerful, why couldn't He just talk to us like an ordinary person? Why did God have to talk to us in such a big, confusing, and boring book? How could I possibly love a God who had such a low opinion of women and girls that he hardly ever even mentioned them in His Word? And how could I love a God who punished people harshly, sometimes big punishments for little things? Like sending Adam and Eve out of the garden of Eden just for eating an apple. He didn't even give them a second chance. And turning Lot's wife into a pillar of salt just because she looked back. There were so many mean things God did to people. I didn't understand how anyone could love a God like that.

I was afraid that God would punish me for the bad things I'd done and the bad thoughts I'd had. I didn't know how to keep God from knowing how afraid I was of Him, because God was supposed to know everything. The best I could do was to pretend I loved God and hope he didn't notice how much I didn't like Him and how afraid I was of Him. But if he found out, he'd probably kick me out of heaven. And that would be scarier than anything.

Most of the time in heaven, God sat on his throne smiling while all who were in heaven told Him how wonderful he was and how much they love Him. But when God got mad, his voice was like thunder, and there was lightning, and God would smite you with all his power. And there was nothing more powerful than God. So the whole time I was in heaven, I would be sitting there scared that God would find out how I really felt about Him. Then he would get mad and smite me with all his power and send me to hell.

As unpleasant as heaven was, hell was much worse. People were thrown into a fire hotter than any fire on earth, like a furnace and a bonfire combined. People were always screaming with pain and fear, and all they got for their screams was more torturing by the devil, who poked them with his pitchfork and laughed his evil laugh, taking delight in their pain because he thought that's what they deserved.

Decades later, when I read Neale Donald Walsch's Conversations with God (Book Two), I would be surprised and immensely relieved when NDW told God his belief that Hitler had been condemned to hell, and God responded that hell does not exist (page 36). God went on to say that, in heaven, we would experience greater peace, joy, and love than we'd ever had in our life on earth.

Upon reading those words, I felt like I could breathe more easily, and I had a sense that my long-festering wounds from the harsh teachings of religion were beginning to heal. But in my childhood, I believed that my only options were an unattractive heaven, an unspeakably horrible hell, and my unhappy life with my parents.

CHAPTER 21

Defending against God

I WAS A TENSE AND NERVOUS child. I can remember waking up at 4:00 or 4:30 a.m. many mornings at age eight or nine, still tired but unable to go back to sleep. And often this happened when I had not had much sleep because I was too tense to fall asleep quickly. I would lie in bed, often with my foot jiggling, alone in the dark, with many thoughts running through my mind. There would always be music in my mental background, tunes I had heard or played or sung. I would have physical memories of playing the piano, roller-skating, sewing by hand, playing jacks with Ruth, and many other activities. I would repeat things learned in school—"i before e except after c," multiplication tables, state capitals. In the background underneath all my mental chatter was my feeling of resentment toward my parents because of their harsh and often disapproving attitudes toward me. And buried underneath everything else was my fear of God, terrified of what God would do to me but having no idea how to get away from Him. I wondered if I was going to go to hell. What would that be like?

I knew that, eventually, I would become an adult and would no longer live with my parents, so I would be able to escape from their harsh methods and unrealistic expectations. That would be a relief. But how could I get away from God? I had been told that God was everywhere, and that God was always watching me. Maybe hell was a place to get away from God. But was it really worth going against my own conscience to do something bad enough to go to hell and being condemned by God and then thrown into a pit of fire and everlasting torment in order to get away from Big Bad God? There must be a better way.

As I was growing up, I occasionally became aware of unnecessary tension I was holding. When I was fourteen, the nurse at camp noticed that, when I was lying down, I was jiggling my foot and seemed tense in other ways. To help me relax, she used an electric vibrator on my back and arms and legs. That was my first introduction to massage. The following year, a new piano teacher made me spend the whole summer doing simple exercises at the piano to relax my arms. When I was twenty, I noticed that my abdomen was habitually tense. At the time I thought it was a good thing, a way of strengthening muscles. I don't think I had lost my earlier fear of God; I had just buried it under the accumulating wealth of knowledge and experiences as I was growing up.

As I look back, I can definitely see the connection between my anxiety and the strict religious principles I was being taught. My parents and Sunday school teachers warned us that we would go to hell if we did not have the right beliefs, but I had trouble understanding what I was supposed to believe. And then I had trouble trying to actually believe what I was supposed to believe.

I didn't want to be like my mother, with permanent worry lines between her eyebrows, her fingers nervously bunching and smoothing the fabric of her dress, and constantly locking doors or anxiously waiting up for children coming home late. She was in the habit of praying every day—often praying out loud, asking God to help with problems and asking God to heal people who were sick. Once I asked her if God answered her prayers. She said, "I'm sure he does," in a way that did not convince me at all. However, it was basically the answer I expected to hear from her. I was very accustomed to what she said being quite different from the feeling I was getting from her.

I learned to deal with my anxiety by glossing over it the best I could. For example, when I first lived alone at the age of twenty-one, I had a fear that someone would break into my apartment and kill me or rape me. After a few sleepless nights worrying about that, I decided I had two choices. If I was going to be raped or murdered (and there was no way I could be absolutely sure that I could prevent a criminal from entering my apartment), I could be raped or murdered in a tense, sleepless state, or I could be raped or murdered in a relaxed, well-rested state. If it was going to happen, I might as well be well rested! After that, I put my worry aside and opted for good nights of sleep.

CHAPTER 22

Live Happily Ever After

HOW COULD I PROTECT MYSELF against Big Bad God? Nobody was going to help me. Certainly not my parents or the other adults around me. They all acted like God was wonderful, and they didn't seem to see how mean and scary He was. I didn't understand how they could not see that. All I knew was that I wanted to protect myself against Big Bad God. I knew that eventually I would die, and then I would have to face Him.

But wait a minute! Maybe I could get married and live happily ever after—just like the princesses in fairy tales. Even though at some level I knew that the stories were not true, I felt comforted in imagining that I could do that. The fairy tale ending, "They were married and lived happily ever after," did not seem any more unbelievable than many Bible stories. Jesus walked on water, a feat that nobody in modern times has been able to do. Jesus fed five thousand people with five loaves and two fishes. God sent manna from the sky for the wandering Israelites. Daniel was unharmed by the lions when he spent the night in their den. Jonah was swallowed by a whale. If I could stretch my credulity enough to believe these things, certainly I could at least pretend to believe that it was possible to get married and live happily ever after.

Of course, at some level I knew that, in real life, many people who were married were not particularly happy and that everyone would die sooner or later. However, my fantasy of getting married and living happily ever after was ever so much more appealing than going to heaven and sitting in front of Big Bad God forever and forever.

I daydreamed about what it would be like to get married. I would wear a beautiful white dress. I would change my name. I would go to live with my husband instead of my parents. My husband and I would love each other and be nice to each other, and he would kiss me on the lips (instead of on the cheek, as we did in my family). We would sleep together, too. He would go to work, and I would stay home and clean house and cook meals. I could choose whatever foods I wanted, and I could do things my way in our house.

Working toward my goal of getting married and living happily ever after, I took care of my appearance. I washed my hair and brushed it a hundred strokes a day. I used curlers and hair clips to arrange my hair attractively. I made oatmeal facials to improve my skin texture. I used Tangee Natural lipstick, and I put Vaseline on my eyelashes to make them shiny. I chose attractive clothes and kept them in good condition (not always easy in that tropical climate!). I learned homemaking skills from my mother—cooking and baking and meal planning, sewing and mending, cleaning and organizing. I tried to cultivate good social skills that I would eventually use in my quest for a husband.

Besides being a way to sidestep heaven, at least in my imagination, getting married was attractive to me in other ways. I would no longer be in my parents' home or subject to their scrutiny. I would be in love with a man, and he would be in love with me. I could not imagine a happier way to live. And once I learned about sex, I looked forward to having sex with my husband. I would be not just allowed but actually expected to have sex with him! After years of prohibition, I would finally have the freedom to enjoy the pleasures of sex. So I expected that marriage would be the answer to almost everything I wanted—independence from parents, permission to have sex, and (in my fantasy) escaping the need to sit in front of Big Bad God for eternity.

CHAPTER 23

Learning about Sex

Princeton, New Jersey, 1955

EVEN AS A VERY YOUNG child I remember being very interested in what I had "down there," what other people had "down there," and the delightful and exciting sensations that could be had "down there." I was strictly forbidden to touch myself down there, and if my parents caught me touching myself, I was harshly punished. I had to keep my interest and curiosity secret, because I was strongly reprimanded for even bringing up the topic or asking a question. My mother told me repeatedly, "Nice girls don't ask questions like that."

I knew that I was not a nice girl, by her definition, but I had to pretend to be a nice girl so that my parents wouldn't give me extra disapproval.

I tried to satisfy my curiosity by undressing my dolls (not very satisfying). Or when I finally had playmates by age five, I would play "doctor" behind closed doors, always being vigilant to avoid trouble with my parents.

By the time I was in elementary school, I knew that babies grew in their mother's stomachs. I had no idea how they got there, and for some time, I assumed that every woman with a big stomach was pregnant.

I saw mothers and fathers around me. I knew that people got married. I heard fairy tales about a prince and princess falling in love and getting married and living happily ever after. That sounded pretty good to me! I thought that falling in love was an emotional thing, which maybe involved kissing. And people who loved each other would get married so that they would be permanently attached. Getting married, in my mind, was a religious ceremony in a church where a man in a suit and a woman in a beautiful white dress would say, "I do." And then they would be husband and wife for life.

Often, married couples had children. I was puzzled. How did it happen that married couples had children? After a while, my thinking went like this: If a man and a woman get married and then live in the same house together, that's all about religion and doing what's proper in society. So, how does the woman's body know that she is married?

After I learned to read, I was searching for information wherever I could find it. The books in our house didn't offer me any satisfaction. There were Bibles, Bible study guides, books of fairy tales (children's version, of course), "wholesome" children's fiction such as Nancy Drew books, and a set of books called The Sugar Creek Gang, about a small group of Christian boys and their adventures. I even looked through a book in my parents' bookcase entitled A Bedouin Lover, but it didn't offer me any new information.

The children's department at the library was similarly sterile. While I enjoyed reading about the Bobbsey Twins and the Wizard of Oz and Raggedy Ann and Raggedy Andy, I had the impression that everyone else had a clean mind, and I was the only pervert around. Sometimes I thought that way, and other times I imagined that most of the children around me were really mainly interested in the mysterious functions "down there" and were only pretending to be interested in other things.

I had been told that, after I turned fourteen, I would have access to the books in the adult section. I fantasized that they were full of the lurid details I was wishing for, but once I reached the proper age to browse through the adult books, I found mostly dry books with scarcely a hint of what I wanted to know. What I didn't know was that any books that were graphic or racy were kept behind the librarian's desk, and one had to ask for them. When I did find out about that, I was not prepared to risk my nice-girl image by asking for them. Besides, the librarian knew my parents.

My best source of information and stimulation was the Sears and Roebuck catalog. Twice a year, we would receive a thick catalog with pictures of thousands of items that could be ordered by mail. In the privacy of my bedroom, I would find the pages with pictures of equipment for enemas and douches, and I would experience a rush of sexual excitement. It was a neat way to circumvent the taboo against touching myself. This was my personal version of pornography. On the same page as the douche bags was a picture of a book titled The Rhythm Way to Family Happiness. I thought it was very odd that there would be a book about a family rhythm band in that section of the catalog, and I thought there might be something about it that I didn't know, but I couldn't ask anyone.

There was much more secrecy about sex and body functions in the 1950s than there is now. For example, in women's magazines, advertisements for sanitary napkins gave only veiled hints what they were about. There would be a picture of a beautifully dressed young woman and, in flowing script, "Moddess … because." And in the grocery store, next to the display of sanitary napkins, there were appropriately sized paper bags so that customers could discreetly hide that item from the inquisitive eyes of children or other shoppers.

In sixth grade, I had the great good fortune to be in the class of Sarah B. Harris. She was the first African American teacher I ever knew. She taught science with gusto, and she understood sixth graders. "You may not sharpen pencils during class, because when you get up to sharpen your pencil, you've probably already been thinking about it for a few minutes instead of paying attention to what's going on in class."

My sixth-grade picture

Once when she was explaining how the digestive system breaks food down, she said, "If you get a cut on your arm and bleed, you don't have peas and carrots coming out through the cut."

I thought that was very funny and started giggling.

"She said, affectionately, "Look at Lizzy laughing back there!"

One day in January, Mrs. Harris said, "Class, I have some books on my desk. When you are finished with your work, I want each of you to come up and take one to your desk and read it. You will get some information you need to know."

One was called Being Born by Frances Bruce Strain, and another was called Growing Up by Karl De Schweinitz. The books were sex education books for children, written delicately but factually by sex education pioneers from the 1940s and 1950s. As I read the books and looked at the pictures, I learned that, in order to make a baby, a man "placed" his penis in a woman's vagina. I was in a state of shock for a few days. What a drastic thing to do! I wasn't even allowed to touch myself down there. How could I ever, in my wildest imagination, let my husband do that to me? How could anyone do it? Wouldn't they be too embarrassed? I realized then that my parents and my grandparents had done that, and apparently they had not been too embarrassed.

On the day they were going to show a film on human reproduction, I was sick and had to stay home from school. I told my mother that I was going to miss the showing of a film on "how babies come about" but that I already knew how it happened. I don't remember how she responded, but I think she was probably relieved that she didn't have to tell me. And of course I was relieved that I didn't have to hear it from her.

The following year, when I was in seventh grade, I hung out with three other girls after lunch, and we often talked about sex, all of us being very curious. None of us had boyfriends, although we each often had crushes on various boys in our school. We wondered how a man and a woman got together, what it was like, and how often they "did it."

One girl said, "I know my parents have done it at least five times, because there are five children in my family.

Another girl wrote this down, which I still find clever and amusing:

The Three Ages of Sex

1. Tri-weekly
2. Try weekly
3. Try weakly

CHAPTER 24

A New Idea to Ponder

Cristobal, Canal Zone, 1955

WHEN DAD WAS AWAY FROM home for several weeks at a time, traveling throughout Central America on business for the American Bible Society, Mom would take over the serious business of reading the Bible to us. One evening when I was eleven years old, she assembled my brother and sisters and me in the living room after dinner, as she often did. We sat on the sofa and the wicker chairs grouped around the edges of the green wool rug. Mom sat on the cushioned easy chair and turned on the reading lamp. She opened her Bible, the ultrathin pages edged with gold, and read to us from Paul's letter to the Romans: "Now the God of patience and consolation grant you to be likeminded one toward another according to Christ Jesus: That ye may with one mind and one mouth glorify God." (Romans 15:5, 6)

As she droned on in her Bible-reading voice (lower and smoother than her regular voice), I watched her soft little double chin bouncing up and down. By this time, I was only half-listening, waiting impatiently for Bible reading to be over so that I could go to my room and finish my homework and choose my skirt and blouse for school the next day. However, just then an unfamiliar word caught my attention: "Now I say that Jesus Christ was a minister of the circumcision for the truth of God, to confirm the promises made to our fathers." (Romans 15:8)

As soon as Mom finished reading and closed the sacred book, I asked, "Mom, what does circumcision mean?"

I'm sure she was wishing that her husband could be there to answer that question, but she had to do it herself. "It's uh … it's an operation on the penis."

I experienced an inner explosion of incredulity and shock, which I tried not to show. I had heard about many strange things in the name of religion, but this was the strangest ever. I knew better than to ask my mother for more information, seeing how embarrassed she had been to tell us that much. However, this made absolutely no sense to my eleven-year-old mind. Operations were performed by doctors in a medical setting, for people who were sick or injured. What did this "operation on the penis" have to do with religion? What could be the purpose of men and boys having this operation that was apparently an important aspect of the Jewish religion of Jesus and Paul? What kind of religion made a practice of performing surgery on male private parts? I thought that religion was about learning to pray, being close to God, hearing Bible stories and learning sayings from the Bible, trying to follow the advice and commandments of the Bible, and having the right beliefs. How was surgery connected with any of that?

I still wonder about it. At my most cynical, I can think that circumcision is a way to have an exclusive boys' club—no girls allowed—and if other guys want to join the club, they have to go through a painful initiation that most would be reluctant to do.

In a different mood, I can think of ritual circumcision as a sign, a symbol, that a man (or the parents of a baby boy) is serious about his role as one of God's chosen people. The Bible tells of God's covenant with Abraham, promising special blessings to him and his offspring and ordering all males of the household to be circumcised. The practice continues to this day among those who consider themselves to be beneficiaries of God's covenant with Abraham, namely Jews and Muslims.

If God is the creator of all things, the source of everyone, and the Supreme Being in the heart of everyone, how could that God choose one group of people as His perennial favorites and demand that they cut off a bit of skin to prove that they are part of His special gang?

Fortunately, I do not believe the Bible is the Infallible Word of God. I see it as a collection of books written by men who may have thought they were inspired but who also included their own prejudices and misinformation, along with whatever truly inspiring messages they may have received. I wonder if they had any idea that their writings would continue to be read, with great reverence, many centuries after they were written. They certainly could not have imagined the various people who would read their writings in lands far away from where they were originally written.

CHAPTER 25

My First Bra

Cristobal Canal Zone, 1956

WHEN WE WERE YOUNG, MY sisters and I were not told what to call certain parts of the body. There was the part that was known as "down there." Or we sometimes called it our "wee-wee place." We also did not have a name for women's breasts, so we called them fat-things. This was not two separate words, as in fat things, but one word said quickly, with the emphasis on fat, as in /FATthings/. And a bra (or brassiere, as it was called by people who dared to mention it at that time) we called a fat-thing cover.

I also had my own private names for some body parts, which I didn't share even with my sisters. I called "down there" my "tee-tee pie," and nipples on men and children I thought of as "beady tops." My father often wore only pajama bottoms for sleeping in the warm, humid climate of Panama, and before he got dressed in the morning, I would see his beady tops. His nipples were small and dark and a little beadier than the pale nipples my sisters and I had. My mother always kept her breasts covered, but I had seen them when she was nursing my sisters as infants, and I knew that she had very long, dark nipples on her very small breasts. She wore a Maidenform 32AA bra, and didn't quite fill it up.

I had gotten the impression from my parents that virtuous Christian women did not emphasize that part of their body. In fact, most of the Christian women I knew had small, unremarkable breasts, and a few had breasts that were solid-looking and matronly. I had the impression that having small breasts was one of the ways these women expressed their modesty and holiness. Good Christian women who happened to have the kinds of breasts that I admired tended to deemphasize them in the way they dressed. Women who flaunted their shapely, attractive breasts were considered worldly, verging on immoral.

When I saw women, especially nice plump women, who had admirable, rounded twin peaks on the front of their upper body, I enjoyed looking at them. I still enjoy the aesthetic pleasure of seeing an attractive woman with shapely breasts. When I was young, I was hoping that I would develop nicely rounded breasts, and I was curious about how that would happen.

Appearance was important to my parents. They insisted on well-combed hair, with haircuts as needed, daily baths, and clothing that was decent and in good condition. I definitely wanted to look good. I wanted to fit in with my classmates, and I hoped my friends found me appealing. In addition, I hoped to get married in due time, and I believed that looking attractive would improve my chances of marrying a good husband and living happily ever after. To support my goals, I worked hard to keep up my appearance. I polished my shoes, ironed my clothes if they needed it, and spent time brushing my hair. I followed recommendations for skin care in Handbook of Beauty from Scholastic Books, and I practiced figure-enhancing exercises every day.

However, I also had a lot of confusion about appearance. How could I continue to try to make myself beautiful without committing the sin of pride? If being a good Christian was the most important thing, according to my parents, why did we put so much effort into looking good? My mother spent an enormous amount of time and energy on appearances. She sewed most of her own clothes and also made clothes for my sisters and me. She washed and ironed. She put Pond's cold cream on her face every night, and she gave herself Toni permanents. I didn't know exactly how my father felt about her efforts to look good, but sometimes when my sisters and I were primping excessively on Sunday morning before going to church, Dad would say, in a loving but slightly disapproving voice, "My beautiful daughters are trying to make themselves look pretty." On the other hand, if I appeared at the breakfast table with my hair uncombed, he said I looked like "a wild woman from Borneo."

There seemed to be certain rules for Christian women. They were to be neat in appearance, and they were expected to be attractively dressed and somewhat in fashion. Especially for church, women wore well-made dresses with a necklace or other piece of jewelry, nylon stockings, and high-heeled shoes. Many women also added hats to their outfit, and each carried a purse and often a Bible. Dresses were supposed to fit well but not conform too closely to the curves of their body, especially the bust and the hips. And necklines must never expose cleavage. Sleeveless dresses or blouses were okay if the armholes fit close enough that nobody could see inside. Sheer blouses were tolerated, as long as there was an opaque slip underneath. All women wore bras and panties and slips, and many wore girdles to rein in some of their bulges.

There are several passages of scripture that give recommendations for women's clothing and appearance. To begin with, Adam and Eve had no idea of covering themselves until they had eaten of the tree of knowledge of good and evil. If they had not eaten the fruit, humans presumably would all be happy nudists. Deuteronomy 22:5 dictates that a woman is not permitted to wear men's clothing. Proverbs 7:10 cautions against "a woman with the attire of a harlot." St. Paul in 1 Corinthians 11 exhorts women to cover their heads and men to uncover theirs when praying or prophesying. He also proclaims that, "If a woman have long hair, it is a glory to her." In his letter to Timothy, St. Paul recommends, "Women adorn themselves in modest apparel; not with braided hair, or gold, or pearls, or costly array" (1 Timothy 2:9).

There were differences of opinion among various Protestant groups as to what were acceptable beauty treatments. Women in our church had their hair cut professionally and sometimes had other treatments at a beauty shop. Almost all these women used some cosmetics, especially lipstick and face powder; however, makeup was to be used in moderation. Sometimes we encountered other opinions. Of the visiting missionaries who stayed in our building on their way to other parts of the world, some approved of treatments that women could do at home but did not approve of having hair cut or permed professionally. Some did not approve of makeup of any kind, which put my mother in a bind. Her Canal Zone friends expected women to wear lipstick all the time, and she wanted to please everyone. I heard her say, more than once, "I wish I could find a lipstick that looks like lipstick to people who think I should wear it and looks like no lipstick to the people who think I shouldn't wear it."

Once, there was a missionary family staying in our building who had a girl about my age. One afternoon, the well-endowed mother asked her daughter to bring her a dress from the clothesline outside. "And the brassiere," she added. That was one of the first times I had heard that word spoken aloud. If my mother had wanted a bra off the clothesline she would have gotten it herself, or she would have said something like, "Bring me the dress and the undergarment beside it." So I was amazed that the visiting missionary spoke so openly and so easily about her brassiere.

In the 1950s, in the community where I lived, most women went to great lengths to conceal their bras. They always wore a full slip over their bra, especially when wearing a dress or blouse that people could see through, and whenever they hung bras or other undergarments on the clothesline outside, they were careful to position them behind sheets or dresses so they would not be seen by passersby.

For children, looking at or talking about underclothing was severely frowned on by adults. In fact, underclothing was sometimes referred to as "unmentionables." Some amusing childhood traditions grew out of this taboo. When a girl would catch a glimpse of her friend's panties, she would say:

> I see London, I see France,
> I see someone's underpants.
> They aren't blue and they aren't pink,
> But my oh my oh how they stink.

Another way that children had fun with this prohibition went like this:

> CHILD 1. Look under there!
> CHILD 2: Under where?

CHILD 1: I made you say underwear!

This was many years before Captain Underpants ever reared his shameless head.

When I was around eleven, I began to notice swelling around my nipples. I was thrilled that I was "developing!" I would soon have my own fat-things! This was an unmistakable sign that I was actually moving toward adulthood. I was hoping that I would have well-shaped breasts that would look attractive, maybe even (did I dare mention the word?) sexy! I certainly hoped they would be bigger than my mother's no-nonsense, strictly practical, baby-feeding breasts. As mine kept on growing, I was proud and excited that my wish was coming true.

After a while they were bouncing up and down on the front of my chest. I fervently wished for a bra. Sometimes I would pull one of Mom's bras out of the clothes hamper and try it on, and once I secretly borrowed one and wore it all day, observing that I filled out her 32AA better than she did. I wistfully looked at the bra display in the commissary when we were on our way to the fabric section or shoe department at the back of the second floor.

I studied the pages of bras in the Sears catalog. There were plain white cotton bras, in sizes from 28AAA to 50DD. Some were stitched in concentric circles to provide better support and a pointier look. The pretty lace-trimmed bras would probably never be seen in our thrifty household; what would be the use of spending extra money for something that nobody was supposed to see? Strapless bras were glamorous and intriguing. How did they stay up without straps? There were padded bras if you wanted to appear bigger than your natural size. For full-figured women, there were long-line bras and foundation garments that combined the functions of a bra and a girdle.

In a special category was "My First Bra," which showed a picture of a pleasant middle-aged woman adjusting the strap of a soft bra on a young teenage girl. I could not picture my mother doing that; she was more likely to hand me a bra in a plain brown wrapper and tell me to try it on in my room with the door closed.

As much as I wanted it, as eager as I was to take this step into womanhood—and stop my fat-things from bouncing around!—I could not bring myself to ask Mom to buy me a bra. It was just too embarrassing to talk to Mom about anything related to the body, especially the parts that had gone unnamed in our home. There was obviously some connection between breasts and sex. And I had learned that having conversation with my mother about anything remotely sexual was extremely uncomfortable for both of us—and something I avoided as much as possible.

When my breasts started to take on their womanly shape and size, I still did not have much of a vocabulary for them. Girls at my stage were said to be "developing," and girls with remarkable breasts were considered "well-developed." I was starting to have a "bust" as it was called in measurements for women's clothing, not just a "chest" as it was called in children's clothing.

Before long, I had two floppy mounds of flesh bouncing up and down on my chest. I wanted a brassiere. I very much wanted one. But I had extremely conflicted feelings about telling my mother I wanted a bra. On the one hand, she was the person who had always taken great care to make sure I had adequate clothing, kept clean and in good repair. When I outgrew my clothes, she made sure I got new clothes, many of which had been constructed on her sewing machine. On the other hand, talking to her about the intimate parts and functions of my body was more than just uncomfortable; it was extremely embarrassing and often shame producing. I cherished my expanding bosom and its message of approaching maturity, and I was very afraid that talking to my mother about a bra would rob me of much of my joy.

And I had even more at stake. Since infancy, I had been severely chastised for any words or actions that had the least bit of sexual connotation. When I asked questions pertaining to sex, I was told that nice girls didn't talk about such things. If my sisters or I uttered a forbidden word, we had our mouths washed out with Ivory soap. I was told to sit with my legs tightly together, with my skirt pulled demurely over my knees (that is, when I was old enough to wear skirts that came past my knees). I was to be careful not to wiggle my hips when I walked. I was not allowed to take dance lessons because dancers showed off their bodies. Having breasts was the most obvious sign that I was becoming a woman, and being a woman gave me great responsibility to stay sexually pure and to be careful not to entice boys or men into immoral acts. Sex, in my conditioned mind, was related to sin, which would lead to hell. Sex, in my private mind, was a glorious, exciting adventure that I was eagerly, though shyly, anticipating.

I even got the impression that my parents, especially my mother, did not approve of me being attracted to the opposite sex. Somehow it was okay for my younger sister Ruth—when she was in fifth grade, talking about Tommy Burroughs, how cute he was, how smart he was, what he said to her, and on and on. Ruth was outgoing and irrepressible. But I was quiet and shy and probably more easily influenced by my parents' attitudes. I got the impression that my parents, especially my mother, wanted me to be so pure-minded that I never thought about sex and never felt an attraction to boys until the right one came along, a righteous man who would love me and marry me. Then, and only then, I could unleash my sexual energy to deeply love the man who would be my husband. I sometimes wondered how it was possible for a sexually repressed woman to suddenly become a sexually satisfied wife as soon as she was married.

I had endured years of being shamed about my body. However, I was very proud of my emerging woman's body, and I didn't know how my mother would react to talking about my newly prominent breasts. I emphatically did not want to be put down, and I was afraid that she would somehow embarrass me.

Finally, after I had endured months of bouncing boobs, one day my mother told me that she was going to get me a bra. This was the moment I had been waiting for! But I couldn't even speak because I was so conflicted between my strong desire for a bra and my fear of being shamed or belittled by my mother. I just paced silently while she told me that she was going to order me a bra from the Sears and Roebuck catalog. She ordered the one called "my first bra," a soft bra of stretchy knitted nylon.

By the time it arrived in the mail a few weeks later, it was barely adequate; it would have fit me better six or eight months earlier. However, I finally had a bra of my own. I was on my way to becoming a woman!

As an adult, I have been happy with breasts that were well developed, not overly large but high and nicely shaped. I appreciated having an attractive bosom, and I was proud of my figure. When I got pregnant, one of the first signs was tender nipples, followed by increased size of my breasts. After childbirth, I thoroughly enjoyed breastfeeding both of my babies. I often had the thought that they were sucking liquid love from my breasts. In my old age, I am still happy to have breasts—they are part of what defines me as a woman. And I am grateful for the pleasure they have given me and my babies and the men I have loved!

CHAPTER 26

Menstruation

ONE DAY WHEN I WAS nine years old, standing in the kitchen, my mother told me in a hushed voice that, when I got a little older, I would have cramps and "something will come out." As she said this, she put her hand on the front of her abdomen. I had an image of "something" oozing out of my abdominal wall. It sounded creepy and mysterious, one of those peculiar grown-up functions that I preferred not to think about.

A few weeks later, my friend Anne shared with me a booklet distributed by a manufacturer of sanitary napkins.

Here is a section from the Kimberly Clark booklet, titled "You're a Young Lady Now":

> One special day you're going to make a discovery. You will notice a stain on your pajamas or your panties. It may happen while you're in bed, or in the bathroom, or at school. It's nothing to be alarmed about because now you know it's going to happen. That little red stain is the first sign that you have started to menstruate.
>
> Menstruation is a flow of watery fluids and a small amount of blood that leaves the body a little at a time over a period of three to five days. It comes from an organ called the uterus or womb which is inside the lower part of your body. When you are married and have a baby that's where the baby will grow. To nourish the baby as it develops, your body builds a spongy lining of blood and watery fluids inside the uterus. When the fluids are not needed they flow away through *an opening in the lower front part of your body.* This happens regularly

about once a month. Then your body begins to build a
new lining for the uterus. This building up and flowing
away process goes on for many years. (italics added)

That gave me a better understanding of what was going to happen
with my body as I grew to be a woman. But I still had no name for
"down there." I had not yet heard of *vagina* or *vulva*. I knew that boys
and men had a penis, which was lacking in girls and women, who only
had a "down there." Now I was learning about something other than
urine that would be discharged from down there. Just allowing that
bloody mess to come out seemed distasteful to me. I fantasized about
training my muscles to hold back the flow until discharging it in the
toilet. If urine could be held, why couldn't menstrual fluid be held?

I had always been very curious about bodies, especially the parts
down there, which my parents did not like for me to talk about or even
ask questions about. So I conducted my search secretly but with little
success. It would be almost a year before I learned the shocking truth
about how a man and a woman come together to conceive a child.

I got my first period when I was eleven. By then, Mom had shown
me where the sanitary napkins were kept, and I had a special elastic belt
to keep a pad close to my body. I was delighted with this signal that
I was indeed growing up and becoming a woman, but I was less than
thrilled with the reality of cramps, stained clothing, and sometimes
heavy flow that required frequent changes of sanitary napkins. (Where
did that term come from?)

When I was in high school in the 1950s, girls could opt out of
participating in physical education class during their menstrual period.
All we had to do was say "regular" during roll call, and we would be
allowed to sit and observe while the non-menstruating girls exercised
their bodies. After seeing how girls in the past used menstruation as an
excuse for inactivity, I now marvel at female athletes (and judges and
professors and ministers and military personnel) who keep right on
doing what they do even at their time of the month.

Over my several decades of menstruation, I tried a number of ways
to deal with it. First came sanitary napkins attached to a belt or pinned

onto my panties. Much later, they came with adhesive backs, making them easier to keep in place. I learned to use tampons, even while I was still a virgin. Later I tried a rubber cup worn internally, and I sometimes used my contraceptive diaphragm to contain the flow. I even tried the old-fashioned practice of using old rags and washing them out. That is a lot of work!

I had a Native American friend who sometimes sat under a tree, bare-bottomed, during her time of the month, allowing the nutrient-rich flow from her body to nourish the earth.

I no longer have to deal with the monthly inconvenience of my menstrual flow. I can't say that I miss it, although I did appreciate the smell, which is no longer part of my life. And it is liberating to be able to wear white pants without the fear that the crotch might turn red.

CHAPTER 27

Women

Mom in fashion show

FROM EARLIEST CHILDHOOD, I ALWAYS "knew", absolutely, without any doubt, that women were inferior to men. And there was no possibility that God would ever love me with the love and respect given automatically to males, simply because I was female. That was just the way it was. There was something inescapably shameful about being female. I could feel that shame, a squirmy feeling of embarrassment and inferiority, in my female parts "down there."

The Bible makes it abundantly clear that women are considered to be vastly inferior to men and much less valuable. It begins with Eve being formed from Adam's rib (rather than being formed by God from the "dust of the ground" as Adam was) to be a "helpmeet" for Adam.

Adam may have been created to make his own decisions and do what he wanted to do, but Eve was created primarily to fulfill Adam's need for companionship.

Then soon after she was created, she proceeded to bring down the whole human race by allowing the serpent to talk her into eating the forbidden fruit and also persuading Adam to eat it. (Well, that's the story, but it definitely did not actually happen that way. We know that humankind developed from a long period of evolution, so the myth of Adam and Eve is just a myth. Even if it would have happened that way, who would have been able to write it down?) The Bible does not say that God blamed Eve for listening to the talking snake and eating the forbidden fruit and getting Adam to eat it, but the story makes it clear that she was the first to succumb to temptation. I got the impression that humanity could have lived perpetually in the beautiful garden of paradise, had it not been for Eve's willful disobedience. That overwhelming burden was then transferred to all women who came after her.

Throughout the whole Bible, men are the interesting characters, the people who do things. And women, if they are even mentioned at all, are almost entirely incidental characters. Even in the genealogies, it is usually only fathers and sons who are named, even though, obviously, there were mothers and daughters, too.

When I was young, I believed that everything about women was inferior—their smelly bodies, their high-pitched voices, their wide hips and bouncing boobs, their preoccupation with food and household chores, their interest in fashion, their gatherings for afternoon tea, their tendency to gossip, the way they walked in high heels, and how they fussed with their hair and lipstick.

I realize now that I had little appreciation for all the things my mother (and many other mothers) did—preparing, serving, and cleaning up after three meals a day, cleaning and arranging things in the house, washing heavy loads of clothing and sheets and towels in a wringer washing machine every week, taking children to doctor appointments and music lessons, listening to children's tales of triumph and comforting them in their pain or grief, and constantly working behind the scenes to keep the household running smoothly. As a child,

I tended to take for granted all the things my mother did, and I often resented her constant work and worry. At least when I was young, I never thought about what was behind the meals that appeared on the table three times a day or the clean clothes I took for granted every morning when I got dressed. And I didn't think about my mother's need for social interaction, perceiving her occasional afternoon tea or her monthly church ladies' meetings as frivolous luxuries.

Men also had smelly bodies, but their smell was different from women's. Men had deep voices and prominent Adam's apple (what a funny name!). Men had to shave the whiskers that grew out of their chins, and a lot of men had hairy arms and chests. The short hair on their heads required nothing more than a quick combing. Men's clothes were very standard—white shirts and dark pants, or overalls for farmers, and a suit for church. They weren't constantly thinking about new clothes the way women were. Men talked about things that women usually didn't talk about—presidents and Congress, taxes and mortgages, events in faraway places, and a lot of other things I didn't understand. People—men and women—tended to pay attention when men talked, but men usually were not interested when women talked.

Women took care of things at home. Men did the important work out in the world.

Women somehow grew babies in their stomachs, and then mothers took care of babies and stayed home with little children while fathers went to work. When fathers were at home, they sometimes talked to their children and occasionally even played with them, but it was mainly the mothers who were with the children.

Doctors were men, and nurses were women. I knew of one exception. In Princeton, we had a pediatrician who was a woman. She visited me at home once when I was sick, looked at my throat, and told me to roll over so she could give me a shot. All the other doctors I knew were men.

When I went to school, almost all of the teachers were women, and most of them were called "Miss" because they were not married.

Radio announcers were men. People listened carefully to them because they knew what they were talking about. Boys delivered newspapers, which had been written by men in newspaper offices.

Of course I knew that I would be a woman when I grew up. I thought about growing up—a lot. I wanted to be able to live apart from my parents. I wanted to have a husband and children of my own. I wanted to be pretty and wear nice clothes.

I didn't think much about what I would do as an adult. Almost all the women around me didn't "do" anything, except take care of their families and the homes they lived in. As a child, I couldn't really imagine doing anything different. I certainly did not want to be a single woman, an "old maid."

My sisters and I had a set of cards for a game called Old Maid. All the other cards eventually formed pairs, but whoever was left with the Old Maid was the loser. The Old Maid card pictured an older woman in a frilly blouse with hair piled on top of her head. She was not pretty, but she was smiling in a way that suggested she was making the best of her unfortunate situation. I knew I did not want to be an Old Maid, the woman that no man would want to marry.

I knew a few unmarried women. My parents were friends with some single missionary women. They seemed to be as actively engaged in converting the heathen as any of the missionary men. I also knew two middle-aged women in our church, sisters, who were not married. They both had protruding abdomens, which I privately called their "proud, child-bearing stomachs," even though I knew that they didn't have children. They seemed to be content with their unmarried status, but I wondered what they did, since they had no family to take care of.

I am now happy and content to be a woman, even when my boobs occasionally get in the way. I enjoy the clothing I wear as a woman, which today is quite different from the way women dressed when I was a child. I am very proud of many members of my gender who have developed their minds and abilities far beyond what women were doing fifty or sixty years ago. Women have accomplished things that we could not have imagined at that time. I still often marvel at women in responsible positions speaking with clear authority. And people—men as well as women—listen to them with great respect. I am grateful for the progress women have made, and I hope and expect that progress to continue.

CHAPTER 28

A Day in the Limkemann Home

Cristobal, Canal Zone, 1956

THE MORNING SUN HAS JUST peeped over the horizon. Swarms of parakeets are chattering noisily in the palm trees outside the open windows of our apartment above Dad's office, the Central American Agency of the American Bible Society. Our pet parakeet, Perry-the-second, squawks in his cage and whistles his name: "PerrEEE! PerrEEE!" I make my way to the bathroom and then head back to my room to put on the pink print dress I have chosen to wear to school today.

From my bedroom window, I can see a ship getting in position to go through the Panama Canal. I hear dockworkers chattering in the street as they head for work at the Cristobal Pier, just two blocks from where we live. As I pass by the door of Mom and Dad's bedroom, I see that Mom is already up, probably in the kitchen, and Dad is sitting on the edge of his bed, wearing only his blue-striped pajama bottoms, with his balding head bowed in prayer and his hands clasped together. I know he will stay there for a few minutes; he never starts a day without prayer, usually also reading from a well-worn New Testament that he keeps close at hand.

He then heads to the bathroom for a quick shower, and I hear him singing:

> Oh God our help in ages past,
> Our hope for years to come;
> Our shelter from the stormy blast,
> And our eternal home.

I can still hear him as I go to the kitchen to pack school lunches and to help set the breakfast table. It's Cream of Wheat with cut-up dates today and grapefruit halves. I put six plastic glasses on the table and fill them with cold water from the jug in the refrigerator. Later I will add four glasses of milk, poured from the glass milk bottle from Mindy Dairy. The milk is pasteurized but not homogenized, so we distribute the cream by shaking the bottle vigorously. Milk is for the children; Mom and Dad have coffee with their breakfast.

Back in the kitchen, I tear off four sheets of wax paper, which I use to wrap four peanut butter and jelly sandwiches on white bread. Each sandwich goes into a paper lunch bag along with a small box of raisins and a few graham crackers. Then I say my table-setting rhyme, "Bread and butter, milk and water," and finish setting the table.

> Mom has been singing,
> "Heavenly sunshine, heavenly sunshine,
> Flooding my soul with glory divine;
> Heavenly sunshine, heavenly sunshine,
> Hallelujah, Jesus is mine,"

her voice going slightly flat on the last notes. The coffee is percolating on the stove, filling the kitchen with its fragrance. Mom dishes out the Cream of Wheat and calls out, "Breakfast time!"

This is the signal for everyone to gather at the table—my older brother, Will; my younger sisters, Ruth and Eunice; and me, Betty, along with Dad at one end of the table and Mom at the end closest to the kitchen. Dad has shaved and put on a clean white shirt for work. Mom has on a flowered apron over her maroon housedress. Ruth is wearing a blue print blouse and a blue skirt. Eunice has on her favorite yellow print dress. And Will has put on a black checked shirt and jeans.

When everyone is seated, Dad leads us in a sung prayer:

> We thank Thee for the sunshine, we thank Thee for
> the rain;
> For food, for home, for life and love we thank Thee
> Lord again.

Once the prayer is done, we can start eating. Eunice goes to get her sunglasses so that she won't get grapefruit juice in her eyes, as the grapefruit halves are likely to squirt their acid juice when we dig our spoons into them. We then eat our Cream of Wheat, along with bread and butter and jelly, if we want it.

Eunice complains, "Mom, Ruth is kicking my chair."

Mom and Dad both give her a look, and Ruth stops.

Will says, "I'm going to Simon's house after school."

Mom says, "Okay."

Eunice says, "I want to go to Rosalind's house after school."

Mom says, "You'll have to wait until after piano lessons. Today is Thursday."

I eat my breakfast and think about meeting Kathleen at school and walking around the halls with her, just to see what's happening. Then it's almost time for the school bus, which will take us to the American school. So we children head out the door and, Dad goes down to his office, leaving Mom with the task of cleaning up after breakfast.

In the evening as we sit down to a meal of roasted chicken, mashed potatoes, green beans, and salad, Dad leads us in a formal prayer: "Our Father in heaven, we are thankful to all be together again. We give thanks for the bounty of food that comes from Thy hand. May it nourish our bodies so that we can serve thee better. We pray in the name of Jesus. Amen."

After supper we move into the living room for Bible reading (this is definitely not optional). We each have a Bible to read or follow along. Dad reads to us from Luke 10:25–37:

> A lawyer stood up to put him to the test, saying, "Teacher, what shall I do to inherit eternal life?" He said to him "What is written in the law? How do you read?" And he answered "You shall love the Lord your God with all your heart, and with all your soul, and with all your strength, and with all your mind; and your neighbor as yourself." And he said to him "You have answered right; do this, and you will live."

But he, desiring to justify himself, said to Jesus, "And who is my neighbor?" Jesus replied, "A man was going down from Jerusalem to Jericho, and he fell among robbers who stripped him and beat him and departed, leaving him half dead. Now by chance a priest was going down that road; and when he saw him he passed by on the other side. So likewise a Levite, when he came to the place and saw him, passed by on the other side. But a Samaritan, as he journeyed, came to where he was; and when he saw him, he had compassion, and went to him and bound up his wounds, pouring on oil and wine; then he set him on his own beast and brought him to an inn, and took care of him. And the next day he took out two denarii and gave them to the innkeeper, saying "Take care of him; and whatever more you spend, I will repay you when I come back. » Which of these three, do you think proved neighbor to the man who fell among the robbers?" He said, "The one who showed mercy on him." And Jesus said to him, "Go and do likewise."

After reading, Dad prays: "Dear Lord, help us to take the teachings of Jesus into our hearts so that we might become better servants for Thee. Help us to remember to do Thy work and to carry Thy word in our hearts that we might not sin against Thee. And, Lord, help all those who are suffering from illness or need. And bless this family and all our loved ones."

Mom adds, "And bless Jake on the trip he is about to go on. Amen."

As soon as the prayer is over, we four children all say, "I didn't know Dad was going on a trip. When is he leaving?"

They tell us that Dad will be leaving the following Monday to be gone for three weeks, one of his regular visits to churches and missionaries in Honduras, Guatemala, Costa Rica, and El Salvador. We know that Dad will send letters to us, handwritten on onion-skin paper and sent by air mail, and Mom will send letters to him at the places where he is planning to stay. But that is a poor substitute for his presence.

CHAPTER 29

Mealtimes

Panama Canal Zone, 1950s

WHEN MEALTIME WAS ANNOUNCED, WE were all expected to come to the table at once—unless someone was officially sick in bed. We had assigned seats, two children on each side, with Mom and Dad at the foot and the head of the table. Eating could not begin until after grace was said or sung. We were taught to bow our heads, close our eyes, and fold our hands together while grace was being said. There were times when one of us girls would tattle on another, "Mom, Eunice didn't have her hands folded!" To which Mom would reply, "Then you must not have had your eyes closed."

There were many times when I did not feel truly thankful for the food in front of me, but I was obligated to join in the prayer of thanks along with the rest of the family. Because this was such a strict rule in our home, I relished the scene in a movie I saw as a teenager. In A Man Called Peter (a biographical film about Peter Marshall, who was a popular minister in the late1940s, serving as chaplain to the US Senate), once when he sat down to lunch with his wife, she asked him to say the blessing. He looked at the bowls of leftovers on the table and declared, "This food has already been blessed."

There were times when I was angry or upset with one or more members of my family, and rather than offer a prayer of thanks, I felt more like joining the author of Psalm 23 when he said, "Thou preparest a table before me in the presence of mine enemies."

After grace, we could begin passing around the bowls and plates of food that Mom had prepared. We each had a glass of cold water; children had glasses of milk and adults had cups of coffee. And there was always bread and butter (or margarine) on the table. For me, eating was a chore, at least until I hit my preadolescent growth spurt. I liked pancakes and waffles (served with imitation maple-flavored sugar syrup), Cheerios, spaghetti and meatballs, tuna noodle casserole, most desserts, and very few of the other mealtime choices.

My mother was definitely not a short-order cook. We children were expected (often cajoled or even bribed) to try a little bit of each food that she served. I grudgingly obeyed, but I had so little enthusiasm for most foods that I often left the table feeling less than satisfied. I had a long list of items of which I unenthusiastically ate only tiny portions—canned peas, lima beans, beets, boiled potatoes, cooked carrots, cooked celery, cooked cabbage, liver, tough beef, fish, and more. Besides disliking many foods, I could not swallow food until I had chewed it very well, and frequently I grew tired of chewing long before I was really full.

Apparently my brother and sisters were not much better eaters than I was, because I remember our mother once exclaiming in exasperation, "I go out and buy food. I cook it. I bring it to the table. Then I throw it in the garbage!"

Once when Dad came home from a trip, he told us about staying at the home of Ralph Rice. He told us that Ralph Rice's children ate with great enthusiasm. I found that very interesting, as I rarely had enthusiasm for eating and could hardly imagine children eating with gusto. I also compared myself unfavorably to those children who were "good eaters."

After breakfast and after dinner, there was almost always Bible reading. Nobody left the table without permission, and if there was to be Bible reading, everyone had to be present. Sometimes children could be excused from the table when they were finished eating, with the clear understanding that they would return promptly when it was time for Bible reading. When Dad was home, he usually selected and read the portion of the Bible for the day.

In midafternoon, Mom often offered us cookies and glasses of Kool-Aid or lemonade. That was something I liked. In fact, I was very fond of cookies and lemonade. But in what seemed to me the reverse logic of my parents, we were not required to thank God for this sweet and tasty snack. I could have offered sincere thanks for that, but somehow that was not part of my parents' religious practice. Thus, I developed a warped sense of gratitude, thinking that I was supposed to be grateful for things I didn't like, but there was no need to be grateful for the little things that I really enjoyed. This added to my perception that Christianity is a religion in which it is more important to say the right words and do the right actions than to express what a person actually thinks or feels in the heart.

CHAPTER 30

Dad

Dad working in his office

I HAVE OFTEN WONDERED IF MY father could have persuaded me to continue being a Christian. He was as devout and enthusiastic a Christian as anyone I've ever met, and he also loved and tried to understand me. However, I did not have a chance to develop much of an adult relationship with him, as he died when I was twenty.

Because he was so immersed in reading and studying the Bible, it was not unusual for him to quote a verse from a psalm at random times during the day, such as, "I will lift up mine eyes unto the hills, from whence cometh my help. My help cometh from the Lord, who made heaven and earth" (Psalm 121:1&2). Or he would say, "The Lord is my shepherd, I shall not want" (Psalm 23). Or he would say it in Spanish, "El Jehovah es mi pastor." He had other favorite Bible verses, such as, "He has shown thee O man what is good, and what does the Lord require of thee but to do justice and to love mercy and to walk humbly with thy God" (Micah 6:8), and, "Whatsoever you do, do all to the glory of God" (1 Corinthians 10:31).

He loved hymns. I would hear his mellow voice singing in the shower:

> When morning gilds the skies, my heart, awaking, cries,
> "May Jesus Christ be praised!"
> Alike at work and prayer to Jesus I repair,
> May Jesus Christ be praised!"

At mealtimes, he often started us singing:

> Praise God from whom all blessings flow,
> Praise Him all creatures here below,
> Praise Him above ye heavenly hosts,
> Praise Father Son and Holy Ghost, Amen.

He usually sang harmony on the amen. He bought a large hymnbook for each member of the family, and we used them often in family hymn singing.

I was the oldest of three daughters. My brother was four years older than me, and Dad had a special relationship with his only son. My relationship with Dad was also special. I can remember Dad carrying me when I was very little, and there were times when he would hold my hand and skip down the hall with me.

Once when I was about six, riding in the car with him, I was chanting, "I-C-E C-R-E-A-M-!" over and over and over. He listened to me for a long time and then said, smiling, "You really like the sound of the words, don't you? And you like ice cream, too!"

When I was a teenager, after being given a ruffled blouse that didn't suit me, he remarked, "I can see that you like to keep things simple— except for your music."

I felt as though he genuinely tried to understand me, and he usually succeeded.

He liked to gently tease my sisters and me by pulling our noses and then showing us his thumb between his fingers to look like a nose. He sometimes told us stories about his childhood, which would usually begin, "When I was a little girl." And we would know he was teasing us.

When Ruth was growing tall and starting to slouch so as to hide her height, Dad convinced her that she would look shorter if she stood up very tall, "because that's what short people do, and by standing tall you will look like a short person." And that actually helped Ruth to stand taller.

Dad liked to play with words. Sometimes her referred to walking as "riding shanks pony." And when I asked him where he went to college, he often responded, "The school of hard knocks." For a while I actually thought there was a school called "Harden Ox." Sometimes when Dad was preparing to take a nap, he would announce, "I'm going to go visit my girlfriend. I'm going to siesta" (see Esther).

Dad was the chief disciplinarian of the family. Mom could handle small infractions of the family rules, but for serious violations she would say, "Just wait till your father hears about this." And when Dad heard about it, he would often give the offender a spanking, which we called "pow-pow." The child would be draped over Dad's knees, with her bottom being assaulted by his hand or, for really bad offenses, with the back of Mom's hairbrush. Ruth was the usual recipient of pow-pow, as she tended to be defiant and oppositional. The rest of us would quietly gloat and smirk, glorying in the fact that it was not us receiving the spanking.

My own grumpy, sullen behavior sometimes led Dad to order me, "Go to your room and stay there until you've made up your mind to act like a civilized human being."

Dad often asked us what we had learned at school, and he also showed an interest in what we were reading. When I was twelve, I thoroughly enjoyed reading The Black Stallion by Walter Farley. Dad skimmed through it and declared that the story symbolized the struggle between good and evil. I could not understand how he came to that conclusion; to me it was purely an entertaining adventure story. I had not yet learned that people tend to give their own interpretation to stories and events.

Although I believe that he probably would have tried to persuade me to remain a Christian, I often think that he would now be glad that I have been able to go beyond Christianity into a practice of deep spirituality that is not limited by the beliefs of a particular religion. He probably would not have been able to make that leap in his lifetime, but I like to imagine that, with the broader perspective of life in the next world, he can appreciate my current spiritual path.

CHAPTER 31

Getting Saved

Panama, 1957

I WAS THIRTEEN YEARS OLD IN 1957 when the famous American evangelist, Billy Graham, came to Panama for a crusade in Panama City. This was a special occasion for my parents, who had high regard for Billy Graham and his ministry. Because going from our home to Panama City involved a difficult two-hour drive, during which one could almost be sure of receiving a traffic ticket from a Panamanian cop on a motorcycle (unless one included a couple of dollar bills when handing him your driver's license), my parents reserved rooms for us in the luxurious Tivoli Hotel, making it a very special occasion. We started with the lavish Sunday evening buffet. In the large, elegant dining room of the Tivoli, there were rows of meats, salads, vegetables, breads, and desserts. And at the center of it was a man in a white chef's hat carving slices of succulent rare beef from an enormous roast. I ate my fill of roast beef, potato salad, fried potatoes, chicken, and fresh warm white bread with butter. Then I helped myself to coconut cream pie and chocolate cake. Even half a century later, I can still remember how wonderfully stuffed I felt, full of more delicious food than I had ever before eaten at a single meal.

We headed for the stadium the following evening after a leisurely day in Panama City. Even though we were there an hour ahead of time, the huge stadium was filling up, and there was a buzz of quiet excitement in the air. Darkness was all around except for the bright lights of the stadium, where I could see more and more people coming to sit expectantly in the bleachers. Soon a singer appeared on stage. It was George Beverly Shea who sang, in a strong, resonant voice, "O Lord my God, when I in awesome wonder, consider all the worlds thy hands have made … Then sings my soul, my savior God to thee, how great thou art! How great thou art!"

After more music, Billy Graham strode purposefully onto the stage. He was a well-built, earnest man with piercing blue eyes, wearing a well-tailored blue seersucker suit. He read from the Bible and talked about the sinfulness of humanity and the need for salvation. "God so loved the world that he gave his only begotten son, that whosoever believes in Him shall have eternal life," he shouted forcefully. "If you want to be saved from the terrible torments of hell, you must turn your life over to Jesus Christ." At the end of each sentence Billy Graham would pause while his translator repeated it in Spanish. Baskets were passed for voluntary contributions.

Then Billy Graham began urging people to come forward to be saved. Insistently, again and again, he urged us to give our lives over to Christ before it was too late. George Beverly Shea led the whole assembly in singing "Softly and tenderly Jesus is calling, calling O sinner come home." I watched as hundreds of people walked slowly toward the stage, many of them sobbing as they went. I wondered if I was really saved. Had I really given my life over to Jesus Christ? Would I be among the fortunate ones who went to heaven to be with all the other Christians who had been cleansed of their sins?

The next evening, giving in to the evangelist's persuasive haranguing, I left my seat and walked toward the stage. I stood back from the crowd, and after a while, my father came behind me and gently steered me toward the large throng who had gathered to commit their lives to Jesus Christ. Soon we were ushered to a backstage area where workers congratulated us and asked for our names and our church affiliation.

Late that night back at home as I undressed in the moonlight, I glowed with spiritual happiness and well-being. I was saved! I knew that I was really saved! That thought gave me great peace and satisfaction. I knelt beside my bed to offer a heartfelt prayer of thanks before falling asleep.

I kept on feeling the glow of salvation. It was lovely, sort of like floating on a cloud.

Our minister, Rev. Franklin, asked me to speak with him in his cluttered office. "I hear you were saved at the Billy Graham campaign.

But we already knew that you are a Christian," he said, with a hint of an indulgent smile. I got the impression that Rev. Franklin had little interest in religious drama. His style was steadier and more down-to-earth, putting one foot in front of the other on the straight and narrow path.

I still continued to feel the glow of salvation. For about two weeks. Then it faded, and I was just my ordinary self and just an ordinary Christian. The experience of getting saved became an echo from my past, similar to the memory of the sumptuous buffet at the Tivoli Hotel—an outstanding experience that had gloriously filled me for a little while until I'd digested it and was ready for further nourishment.

After that, I began wondering if I was still saved. I wondered what "being saved" really meant. I wondered about the various practices and traditions of people who called themselves Christian. There were Catholics, who recited long memorized prayers. There were Protestants, who made up spontaneous prayers. Some churches were very strict about Bible interpretation, and others were more lenient. Some groups of Christians rigorously refrained from dancing or drinking, and others included drinking and dancing at church social functions. Apparently there wasn't a "right" way to be a Christian.

So, what did it really mean, that I "got saved" at the Billy Graham campaign? Had I just given in to the pressure that he created by telling us that we needed to give our lives over to Christ or risk going to hell? He had been very persuasive, and I had felt sincerely called to submit to Christ. Or had I? Was I just following the crowd, not wanting to be left out of a dramatic experience? Or, more in keeping with my personality, was I just doing what I believed I was expected to do? I had felt enormous pressure to "go forward" and experience salvation. Billy Graham was so insistent and so believable to my young Bible-fed mind that I could scarcely resist.

But now that the glow had faded, I was confused. I didn't know what was real and what was imaginary. An important question was beginning to form in my mind: Were Christians the only people who would be spared the horror of everlasting hell? In due time, that question would lead me to a life-changing realization.

CHAPTER 32

Summer with Grandma

THE SUMMER I TURNED FOURTEEN, my whole family stayed with Grandma Peters in her small house in Wesley, Iowa. Wesley was a town of about five hundred people in northwest Iowa, surrounded by cornfields. There was a post office and a general store downtown, and a train went through several times a day. It was even possible to get on or off the train in Wesley by making arrangements for a "whistle-stop." Grandma had moved there from Missouri after her husband died so that she could be near her son Harry, who had a farm nearby. Uncle Harry was a hardworking, loud-talking farmer with a wife and three small children. He went to see his mother several times a week, often bringing his family along.

We settled into Grandma's two-bedroom house as well as possible. Grandma had her own bedroom, of course, and Mom and Dad slept in the other bedroom. Ruth and Eunice slept on a pull-down sofa in the living room, where I slept on a hide-a-bed. Will slept on an army cot on the screened-in porch. During the day, I often practiced on the old upright piano that was kept on the porch. My big project that summer was learning the fast movement at the end of Beethoven's Moonlight Sonata.

It was a summer of memorable food. Grandma baked large loaves of white bread at least twice a week, punching down the dough with her arthritic thickened wrists. She also baked excellent pies, including blueberry—my dad's favorite—and lemon meringue. For my fourteenth birthday in July, she baked her traditional angel food cake, from scratch. She had a vegetable garden where she grew a variety of vegetables. What I remember best was the light green frilly leaf lettuce, which she liked to serve sprinkled with sugar and a few drops of half and half. We had wonderful tomatoes and green beans that summer and as much corn on the cob as we could possibly eat, fresh from the nearby cornfields. In addition to the vegetable garden, she also had a row of colorful pansies near the back door of her house.

Grandma was in the habit of rising early and lighting a fire in her corncob stove (the fuel was, literally, dried corncobs—very plentiful in that part of Iowa). She usually had CocoWheats for breakfast, often with homemade bread and homemade jam.

Grandma had a plaque that I saw every time I went between the living room and the kitchen. The plaque read:

> Only one life, 'twill soon be past.
> Only what's done for Christ will last.

Grandma's idea of doing something for Christ apparently did not include Catholics.

Unfortunately, the only girl my age within walking distance was a Catholic girl named Janet. Grandma would have preferred for me to get together with a girl who went to her church. However, since the girl lived several miles away and I had no way of getting together with her, Grandma relented and allowed me to spend time with Janet, who was a lovely, friendly girl who was planning to become a nun. My brother liked her, too, and once asked her on a date. Her parents allowed her to go only if her younger sister and I accompanied them.

During the day, especially in nice weather, my sisters and I often played with the kids living on a nearby farm. Will had a summer job de-tasseling corn—it had something to do with preventing cross-pollination of hybrid seed corn. We all tried to find ways to entertain ourselves so we wouldn't bother Grandma too much. I can imagine that it was challenging for her to suddenly have six people, including children, living with her.

Grandma's house was on a gravel road about a mile from town. I often walked to town or to Janet's house, and I always passed by a house on the other side of the road where a boy my age and his older brother were often working on cars in the yard. Sometimes they would whistle at me as I went by. Grandma didn't think very highly of that family.

One day I got up the nerve to go across the street and actually talk to the boy. His name was Dean, and he was nice-looking and friendly.

After a brief visit, I said goodbye and went back to Grandma's house. Grandma and Mom had been looking out of the kitchen window and had seen what I had done. This was not okay with Grandma. I'm still not quite sure what she objected to. Did she think I was being very forward and flirting excessively? Was it because she didn't like Dean's family? (Maybe she thought of them as "poor white trash." She certainly was not wealthy, but she was educated and very proper.) Maybe she just wanted control of what I did and who I associated with. Whatever the reason, I was grounded for two days and not allowed to leave the yard. Amazingly, while I was sitting on the front steps with my sisters, Dean came over and sat beside me. We even brushed hands!

After that I was careful to try to appear virtuous as far as Grandma was concerned, even though she was hard to please. Her standards were even more rigid than my mother's, which is saying a lot. My brother has characterized Grandma as "severe and uptight." Over all, however, I have mostly happy memories of that summer.

CHAPTER 33

A Welcome Discovery

Cristobal, Canal Zone, 1958

ONE WARM SATURDAY AFTERNOON WHEN I was fourteen, I went into the bathroom while my parents were sipping lemonade in the living room with some visiting missionaries. Seated on the toilet, with my bare feet resting on the cool tile floor beside the claw-foot bathtub, a revolutionary idea came to me: If God loves everyone, then God loves Hindus and Jews and Muslims and Buddhists and even atheists, not just Christians!

This was a new and earthshaking thought for me. All my life I had been told that Christianity was the only way to salvation. I had been told that "God so loved the world that He sent His only son, that whosoever believes in Him will have eternal life" (John 3:16). And Jesus had proclaimed, "I am the Way, the Truth and the Life. No one comes to the Father except through Me" (John 14:6). Could it possibly be that this was not the whole Truth? Was it possible that there could be other ways to salvation and heaven besides what the Bible promised? Was it really possible that there was nothing we had to do and there were no requirements to be loved by God? He just loves us the way we are! What a comforting and exciting thought!

This did not feel like the Big, Bad, Mean, Scary God who seemed to be behind so many events in the Bible. This was a loving and lovable, warmly accepting God. Maybe He even loved females as well as males. He probably did—if He even loved atheists who didn't even believe in Him! This was an extremely bighearted God who loved everyone and didn't care what we believed. Wow! What a revelation!

This felt truer than anything had ever felt to me. It felt not just true in the same way as 2 + 2 = 4 but like a much higher order of Truth.

I did not want to risk letting anyone try to talk me out of this—especially my parents. I certainly didn't think that they would be able to accept a God who loved everyone—Hindus, Buddhists, Catholics, people who could be going to church but chose not to, and even atheists! My parents were deeply invested in believing that Protestant Christianity was the way to salvation, and they had spent years in Honduras and endured great hardships to spread the Good News of the Gospel and lead others to the true way as they saw it.

But how could it be true that Christianity was the only way if God really loved everyone, regardless of his or her beliefs? I was quite sure that, if I told my parents about my revelation, they would try very hard to discredit it and would try again to convince me that their way was the only way. I did not want to risk that. The thought that had come to me felt more real and truer than any thought that I had ever had before. I decided that I would not tell anyone what I had experienced, because I was quite sure that all the people around me were similarly brainwashed and would not understand.

By the time I had washed my hands and left the bathroom, I knew that I did not dare to speak about the idea that had come to me. And I also knew that I would carefully nurture it and treasure it in the secrecy of my heart.

In my family, Christianity was not just a religion; it was a total way of life. My father, an ordained Presbyterian minister, read passages of the Bible to us every morning and evening. My mother's father had also been a minister, and both parents had grown up in families focused on reading the Bible and going to church. We had prayers before meals and after Bible reading. My brother and sisters and I went to church every Sunday with our parents, clutching our well-worn Bibles and our well-prepared Sunday school lessons. We participated in all church functions, including rummage sales, picnics, and youth rallies. My father worked for the American Bible Society and traveled throughout Central America promoting the use of the Bible. We often had visiting Christian missionaries staying in apartments in our building, and my parents frequently entertained missionaries and other religious workers.

I had always been taught that Christianity was the one and only way to reap the benefit of everlasting peace and joy in heaven. Maybe, just maybe, God would be merciful enough to make an exception for people who had never had the opportunity to hear the Gospel of Jesus Christ. But I understood that there would be no leniency for people who had heard the Gospel and rejected it. I could definitely believe that the prejudiced and intolerant God of the Bible could keep people out of heaven if He judged that they did not have the right beliefs

That was one of several things about Christianity that I could not accept. I longed for a God who would be more merciful than to condemn to hell those who did not believe in Jesus. I had been told that Christians were saved from hell because Jesus had died for our sins. I tried and tried but could never understand how Jesus had died for my sins many centuries before I was even born.

I had lived with a constant undercurrent of depression and hopelessness because I absolutely believed that, as a female, no matter what I did or thought or felt, I would never be loved by God with the natural, automatic love that God had for men and boys. The message I received from the Bible, over and over, was that men were important, and men did important things, and women had so little value that they were usually ignored as if they didn't even exist.

However! If it was really true that God loved everyone, then I no longer had to believe everything that I had been so carefully taught. I didn't have to believe that Jews were God's chosen people. I didn't have to believe that only properly baptized Christians could go to heaven. I could even dare to believe that God loved females just as much as He loved males! And I could start believing in a God who was kind and loving and accepting of everyone—not the wrathful, punitive God I had read about in the Bible. I knew at some level that I had just discovered a truth more profound than I had ever encountered. I also knew that I could not talk about this with my parents, because their minds had been completely indoctrinated many years previously, and I was sure that they would try to cast serious doubt on what I now knew to be absolute truth. I knew, too, that, as long as I lived with my parents, I had no choice but to try to be a good Christian. Although I kept my discovery quietly to myself, I felt comforted and assured that I knew, privately, about something much better than Christianity.

CHAPTER 34

Teenage Christian

Cristobal, Canal Zone, late 1950's

AS A TEENAGER, I BECAME increasingly aware of my parents' expectations for me to be a good Christian. Some aspects were not difficult. Following the Ten Commandments, at least some of them, had become second nature to me. I could easily refrain from killing, stealing and committing adultery. As for not taking the Lord's name in vain, children in my family were not allowed to say "gosh" or "gee" because they sounded too much like God and Jesus, so we used words like "darn" and "heck" and "boy-oh-boy."

More difficult was the greatest commandment: "Thou shalt love the Lord thy God with all thy soul, with all thy strength, with all thy mind." Was I supposed to be passionately in love with the Big Man in the Sky? I had no idea how to do that. My teenage image of God was of an old man in a long white robe with lots of white hair; a long white beard; a fierce, gravelly voice; and tobacco-stained teeth. I'm not sure where the image of tobacco-stained teeth came from, but that was how I pictured God. Underneath His long white robe He had a penis. And I knew this God-with-a-penis did not like women very much, as He usually paid little attention to women throughout most of the Bible. So I could not find a way to love this God, although I tried to pretend that I did.

There were other biblical principles that I carefully attempted to follow. One was the Golden Rule: "Do unto others as you would have them do unto you." Thinking about that saying, I decided I needed to modify it, because I knew that the way I wanted to be treated was not necessarily the same way every other person wanted to be treated. So I tried to adapt that rule to fit real people in my life.

One of my father's favorite verses was Micah 6:8: "He has showed thee, O man, what is good, and what doth the Lord require of thee but to do justly, and to love mercy, and to walk humbly with thy God." That sounded good, and it was broad and general enough to mean to me that I should strive to do the right thing in every situation. As for walking humbly with my God, I wasn't sure how to do that, so I ignored that part of the verse.

When I studied Philippians 1:10, "that ye may be sincere and without offense till the day of Christ," I interpreted that to mean that I should use deodorant!

I unfortunately took to heart Paul's advice in Philippians 2:3–4: "Do nothing from selfishness or conceit, but in humility count others better than yourselves. Let each of you look not only to his own interests, but also to the interests of others." I tried diligently to consider others better than myself and to be aware of their interests. People around me seemed to be happy to let me do that. As I was apparently the only person in my circle following this advice, I found people taking advantage of me. I wished that others would look to my interests as well as their own. But nobody else seemed to be following that advice, so I ended up feeling less than anyone else. Added to my naturally shy and self-effacing personality and my perception that as a female I should always have a higher regard for males, this contributed to my tendency to be a shrinking violet.

In addition to the Bible, I was tremendously influenced by hymns, especially because I always had tunes running through my mind, and usually the words came along with the tunes. Some were very positive for me, such as "Spirit of God, descend upon my heart." and "Breathe on me, Breath of God, fill me with life anew, that I may love what Thou dost love and do what Thou wouldst do." It was much easier for me to appreciate God as a spirit rather than the negative physical images I had of God the Father. I appreciated the reverence of feeling God's spirit in my heart. Once, at summer camp, I went alone into the chapel and felt the Presence of God in a deeply emotional way. The feeling did not last long, but it helped to convince me that there was something there.

There were other hymns that did not seem so positive to me. "When the roll is called up yonder I'll be there" seemed to emphasize the rift between the "saved" and the "unsaved." After my experience at the

Billy Graham campaign, I had a lot of confusion about what it meant to be saved, and I was uncomfortable with the attitude of some people considering themselves saved while others were presumed to be doomed to an indescribably horrible afterlife. To me, that seemed even more unfair than many of the supposed actions of God in the Old Testament.

I could sing the very familiar words and tune of "Onward Christian Soldiers," but if I thought about its military aspect, I felt uncomfortable about fighting in the name of Jesus. And I wondered who we were supposed to be fighting against.

I became increasingly involved with church as a teenager. I sang in the choir, going to choir practice on Wednesday nights, and changing into my choir robe in the ladies' room before church on Sunday mornings. Sunday school lessons for teens were complex and required careful preparation. I went to youth fellowship on Sunday evenings and occasionally to youth rallies with teenagers from other churches. I started playing the organ for the early Sunday morning service at the Coco Solo chapel. And when Mrs. Genis moved away, when I was fifteen, I became the organist for our church. This entailed practicing hymns and preludes and postludes every week and generally spending more time at church.

I thought of Christianity as the "default" religion. Of course, if you wanted to be in a religion, Christianity was the obvious choice. I had been taught that Protestantism was the "right" form of Christianity, and the Roman Catholic Church with its Pope and priests and nuns was the "wrong" form.

Even within Protestantism, there were many variations. I went to school with Reba, Mary-Esther, and Joanne Jones, whose parents were ministers of the Nazarene Church. The girls dressed very modestly and did not wear any makeup or jewelry, unlike other girls at school. They sat together at lunch and had long prayers before they opened their brown paper bag lunches. They were pleasant and friendly with me but always seemed to hold themselves aloof from the general student body. My friend Carol Agee went with her parents to the Episcopal church, where they recited long, wordy prayers out of a prayer book. Carol Seaman went to a Catholic church, where they dressed casually and covered their heads and made the sign of the cross. There were some denominations that practiced infant baptism and others that insisted on baptism of adults only. I didn't understand their differences; I only knew what was familiar and comfortable to me.

Ruth and I occasionally talked about religion. Once we had a discussion about a family prayer that we often said before meals. It included the phrase "make us ever kind and good." I interpreted that as faking goodness, sort of a mincing goody-two-shoes goodness. She said, "No! Make us ever kind and good!" as she pounded her fist on "kind" and "good," indicating that those were very strong and positive attributes and goals to strive for.

And of course I had a somewhat normal teenage life. I went to school, did my homework, practiced piano daily, and surreptitiously listened to the hit parade with my bedside radio turned low. (My parents disapproved of popular songs.) I was a Girl Scout. I got together with my girlfriends, occasionally going to a movie. My parents would reluctantly give me permission to see a movie if Parents magazine approved it. Once I saw a movie without their permission, and I have wished ever since that I hadn't seen it. It was Vincent Price's The House of Wax, my first horror movie. I had nightmares for a long time after that.

More than once, I asked Dad, "What's so great about the Bible?"

He answered enthusiastically, "It's a collection of history, poetry, and prophecies. And it tells the story of God's people, including the deeds and teachings of God's Son, Jesus and the remarkable deeds of the early Christians. Here, let me show you some outstanding words of wisdom found in the Bible." And he showed me how to carefully underline key passages in the Bible. He gave me a hardbound copy of the Holy Bible, Revised Standard Version, including references, and he showed me how to use the references where one verse in the Bible is related to a verse in a different part of the Bible.

When I was inspired to try to be a good Christian, I would sometimes open my Bible and read a portion and try to apply it to my life. I would also pray for understanding.

I wanted to be good. Once I set a goal for myself—to get rid of the "sinful feelings" of pride, anger, and resentment. I didn't understand that those feelings could not be eliminated and that even my uncomfortable emotions served a purpose. The point is that I wanted to be a good Christian.

But I had my limits. One Saturday morning after breakfast, as Dad was reading to us a particularly long passage from the Bible, the phone rang. I started to get up to answer it, and Dad said, "Whoever it is can wait. Nothing is more important than this."

I did not dare disobey him, but I felt very agitated, with my thoughts far from Holy Scripture. I was thinking, in dramatic teenage fashion, What if that was my secret admirer finally getting up the courage to call me? What if he never again had the courage to call me? Maybe he was the one I was supposed to marry. So now I would never have a chance to get married and live happily ever after—all because of the stupid Bible!

Somewhere in the background behind church and the Bible, there were questions forming in my mind that I did not dare ask my parents or even my friends. If Christianity was the only way to salvation, why didn't everyone want to be a Christian? If I really loved the Bible as the Word of God, would it seem less dreary and less confusing? Why did the God of the Bible seem to be so prejudiced against women and certain other people? These questions nagged at me for many years. I thought that, if I found satisfactory answers for them, I would be able to be united with my parents in their religious beliefs, which was something I really wanted.

In spite of decades of searching, I have never found satisfactory answers.

CHAPTER 35

Going to College

Panama Canal Zone to Wooster, Ohio, 1961

Our last family picture, taken before I left for college

I ASSUMED THAT I WOULD GO to college after graduating from high school. This was what most of my high school friends were doing as a matter of course, and I saw it as the logical next step for me. My brother was in college, and my father was well educated, having completed college, seminary, and a master's degree in theology. But I was one of the first women in the family to even consider a college education. My maternal grandmother had been trained in a short course at a county normal school to be a schoolteacher, which she was until she married at the age of twenty-nine. None of my other female relatives had gone beyond high school. But I had the opportunity. My academic skills were adequate. I didn't need to find a job right away. And best of all, my tuition was being paid by my father's employer, the American Bible Society.

I eagerly looked forward to going to college, not so much because I was interested in learning and studying but because I would be far away from my parents. For the first time in my life, I would be free from their scrutiny, their restrictions, and their frequent disapproval. I would be living among other young people; I would be free to choose what I wanted to study, who I wanted to socialize with, and how I wanted to spend my spare time.

And, secretly, I hoped to find a husband. I knew that lots of young women went to college more interested in becoming a Mrs. than in getting a bachelor's degree. But for me, getting married had an additional purpose, which I had never told anyone. Getting married and living happily ever after was my plan to bypass the aspects of heaven that, in my imagination, seemed so very unattractive. Finding a husband was my alternative to having to spend eternity with Big Bad God. Even though I knew it was a fantasy, I clung to it as the happiest outcome I could imagine.

I had spent months preparing my wardrobe. My thin cotton dresses were fine for summer and the heat of the tropics, but I was going to experience cool and even cold weather. As I was accustomed to sewing most of my own clothes, I cut and sewed a lovely wool skirt and found a sweater to coordinate with it. I made several dresses that I thought would be suitable for class, but when I got to Wooster, I discovered that they were better suited for wearing to church or on dates.

I wasn't sure what subject I wanted for my major area of study. I had a secret interest in psychology, but I didn't dare even mention it to my parents. They had often made remarks about following Jesus and the Bible and not relying on human help, which they would probably consider to be misguided, especially if it was not anchored in the Bible.

The most logical area of study for me would be music, as I had gained skill and experience studying piano for ten years and playing the organ at church for three years. That is in fact what I studied. What I learned as a music major has enabled me to have a long and satisfying career as a musician.

I threw myself into college life. My assigned roommate, Joan, was compatible and pleasant, and there were interesting young women around us. I diligently attended classes and completed my assignments as well as possible. I enjoyed chatting with other students, and I was thrilled to finally start dating. I had had only two or three dates in high school, as I was shy around boys, and I felt very uncomfortable even hinting to my parents that I was interested in boys. In college I went out with a variety of young men, going to dances and concerts and occasional movies. My life had definitely taken a turn for the better.

CHAPTER 36

Badgered into Getting Saved—Again!

Wooster, Ohio, 1962

STANDING BY THE COATRACK BY the college dining hall after my evening meal, I turned as a young man approached me. "Hi! I'm John Oldhouse! I don't think we've met."

I was a sophomore and I learned that he was a senior. This did not feel like a flirtation, and that was fine with me. I was interested in guys who were nice-looking but not overly handsome, who had interesting things to say, and who also were interested in what I had to say—guys who were smart but not too brainy. He didn't seem to fit into any of my preferred-male categories.

Soon he got to the point of his introduction. "Are you a Christian?" he asked.

"Well, yeah." I squirmed. "My parents were missionaries, and I was raised in a Christian home."

He replied, "That's all well and good, but I want you to know that God has no grandchildren. We each have to work out our own salvation with fear and trembling." He motioned me toward an empty stairwell, where we sat as he continued to talk. "All have sinned and fall short of the glory of God," he said, pulling out his Bible and showing me the verse. "I suppose you know John 3:16."

"Yes," I replied. "'God so loved the world that whosoever believes in Him should not perish but have eternal life. For God sent not his son into the world to condemn the world, but that the world through Him might be saved.'"

I was hoping that he would be satisfied and end the conversation. This was not to be. He continued impressing on me the need for salvation, telling me it was urgent that I commit my life to Christ. Finally, as I could see no other way to end the conversation, I agreed to pray with him and to accept Jesus Christ as my personal savior. I did so but with many doubts and misgivings.

However, this was not the end. Not yet. He said, "Now we need to go share our good news."

He walked with me across campus to the InterVarsity office, a do-gooding conservative Christian organization that I had studiously avoided. As he ushered me in, he said to the two girls in the sparsely furnished office, "We have some good news for you. Tell them what it is."

I told them shyly, "I have accepted Jesus Christ as my savior."

"Oh, how wonderful," they gushed, with excessively bright smiles.

I knew several students who were involved with InterVarsity. They impressed me as being clean and pious and righteous. They were the ones who silently bowed their heads for long moments before each meal in the campus dining rooms. They carried Bibles around with them, and they were eager to talk about the love of God and the need for salvation. I had quickly learned not to get into a theological discussion with them, because they always knew some obscure verse from the Bible that would "prove" that my point was invalid. How could any of my puny thoughts or objections stand up to the "truth" written within the Word of God?

I mostly avoided being around them. I did not appreciate their insufferable cheerfulness. I did not enjoy conversations that were filled with scriptural quotations, proclaimed as if God Himself had spoken directly to them. I was beginning to entertain doubts about the sacredness and authenticity of the Bible, and I did not want to be squelched by their one-sided, heavy-handed, and overly facile insistence on the benefits of the Bible and their own interpretation of it.

At last I was free to go back to my dorm, feeling embarrassed and a little shaken and full of questions. Why were they so eager for me to be saved and to declare my acceptance of Jesus as my savior? What was in it for them? I had always considered my beliefs and my relationship with God to be a very private affair, and I often felt embarrassed when people prayed out loud around me. Why were religious people so insistent on getting others to accept their beliefs and point of view? And was there any real benefit to people like myself who were badgered into accepting someone else's brand of religion without really believing it?

I still wonder about that. Why is it so important to religious people to convince others that their religion is the best? I've been around Mormons, Jehovah's Witnesses, and fundamentalist Christians who have all tried to convince me that their religion was the only religion worth believing. And I know that there are millions of Muslims who are convinced that theirs is the only valid religion. They can't all be true, can they? Why can't everyone just be content to believe what they believe, live their lives according to the best principles they know, and let others do the same? I wonder if there is maybe a seed of doubt within them that continues to bother them as long as there are people around them who haven't accepted the same beliefs. Maybe knowing that someone does not accept their beliefs as God's Truth opens the door to a little bit of doubt. And maybe that little bit of doubt creates some discomfort in them. Many people feel most comfortable being around other people who have similar beliefs. Maybe I could take it as a compliment that they want to share their beliefs with me. But I don't enjoy the heavy approach that many religious people use.

I also had basic questions for myself. What qualities could I develop so that I could engage in meaningful conversation with people who had deeply entrenched beliefs? What kinds of attitudes would I need in order to hear what people had to say without feeling like I had to believe what they believed? How could I protect myself from people who were overly aggressive about their beliefs?

An even more basic question was this: Why am I so easily swayed by people's religious arguments? I think there are several reasons. To begin with, I am never 100 percent sure that my beliefs and opinions are correct. I always want to check up on myself because I know I'm fallible and prone to error. So, when someone tells me something they believe that I may not have considered, I tend to wonder if there is some truth in what they are saying that I may have overlooked before.

This is sometimes a rather cumbersome way to live. Even decades after I had rejected the Christian beliefs of my parents, occasionally my attention would be caught by an article or a book that seemed to offer a new way to explore and explain away the problems I was having. I would get my hopes up, time after time; maybe this article, this lecture, this book, would at last explain Christianity to me in a way that I could accept.

I fervently wished to be united with my parents in the sureness of their beliefs. I would have liked nothing better than at last to understand and fully agree with their passion for the Bible and their Christian religion. Time after time I read an article or listened to a talk that might possibly hold the key to understanding and accepting Scripture and the religion based on it. Time after time, I was disappointed. I found nothing that could convince me that the Bible was absolutely true, that the God of the Bible was worth loving, and that the beliefs of the Christian church were logical or believable. In early adulthood, I came to the conclusion that Christianity was not for me, and I have never found a suitable argument to take me back to Christianity.

I also wonder about my father's career as a Christian missionary. What fueled his enduring enthusiasm for saving souls? Did people feel badgered when he talked to them about Christianity? I will never know. However, I like to think that his usual friendly, respectful attitude was also part of his approach to missionary work. Although he was often quiet and thoughtful, he seemed to genuinely enjoy meeting new people and easily struck up a conversation. He liked to make jokes and laugh, and his good humor often helped to ease the way. Although he was well educated, he had grown up as a farm boy, so he was comfortable with a wide range of people. I like to think that, when he met someone he considered a prospect for conversion, he got to know something about the person before leading him or her into a conversation about the Bible and Jesus. I do know that, during his lifetime, he had the reputation of being a particularly effective missionary. And I know that many of the missionaries and Central American people who had met him had fond memories of him.

Dad shaking hands with a man in Honduras

CHAPTER 37

Terry

Wooster, Ohio, 1963–1966

WHEN I WAS A JUNIOR piano major at the College of Wooster, Terry entered as a freshman organ major. I would often see his tall frame bent over the pipe organ keyboard as I passed by his practice room window. And I could hear him diligently practicing Bach fugues as I returned to my piano practice room to play Beethoven and Mozart sonatas. He liked to make puns; he would often tell organ players to "pipe down" or say that their playing was "great" or "swell" (great and swell being names commonly given to divisions of a pipe organ, with their corresponding separate keyboards).

A few months after we met, he invited me to a college dance. As we danced, he told me about his hobby, photographing and measuring old wooden covered bridges, which were not common but could still be seen at river crossings on obscure country roads. He told me much more about covered bridges than I really wanted to know, and I decided that I would not go out with him again. However, a few weeks later when I wanted a date for a college folk music concert, I agreed to go with him.

We had light conversation on that cold February evening as we walked a few blocks to the high school gym where the event was being held. We found seats high up in the bleachers. After the folk singer finished, Terry took my hand as we stepped down the wooden bleachers, and I had a rush of warm, almost maternal feelings.

When we arrived at my dorm, he pulled a small heart-shaped box of chocolates out of his coat pocket and, with a slightly cracking voice, said, "This is for you. Happy Valentine's Day," as he handed it to me. Then he asked, "May I kiss you goodnight?"

I nodded, and we kissed.

After he left, I went upstairs to my room with the excited feeling of being in love.

After that, we were together most weekend evenings, and we often walked hand in hand on campus or in nearby parks, talking, laughing, and kissing. We went to concerts and lectures together and had many conversations about everything.

When I told Terry that I had received word from my mother that my father had been operated on for a malignant tumor, Terry said, in his blunt way, "Oh, that means your dad has cancer."

As soon as classes were over, I went to spend the summer with my parents and sisters. They had recently moved from Panama to Mexico City, where my father had a new job, still with the American Bible Society. While I was with my family that summer, Terry and I wrote frequent letters to each other. I shared my thoughts and feelings on paper, and I eagerly anticipated his letters.

My father died in November, and Terry never had a chance to meet him. A few months later, I invited Terry to visit with my mother and sisters during a college vacation. He got along well with them.

Within the year, we began to talk about marriage. He had thought that he would not marry until he completed his education (PhD), but I wanted to get married soon. We decided that we would marry the year before his senior year of college, which was a year after my graduation.

Yippee! I was on my way to getting married and living happily ever after!

CHAPTER 38

Dad's Illness

Mexico City, August 1964

"BETTY, LET'S GO TO YOUR room. I need to talk to you," said Mom in a strained, urgent voice. She had just returned from meeting with Ray Strong, who had come to Mexico from the American Bible Society office in New York City.

After we were seated on my bed in my small bedroom on the second floor of our house in Mexico City, she said, "Tonight, Ray Strong told me that he has seen Dad's medical records, and his prognosis is not good. Although the doctor in New Orleans told Dad to go home and have physical therapy to get his strength back, the doctor really doesn't expect him to live much longer."

I was stunned. I said, "Have you told Dad what you learned?"

Mom replied, "Ray thinks it is up to the doctor to tell him."

I disagreed. "I think we should tell him."

Mom replied that she would leave it up to the doctor to tell him.

Dad had not been feeling well for several months earlier in the year, and when Mexican doctors could not find his problem, Mom went with him to the Ochsner Clinic in New Orleans. After several days of tests, suddenly Dad became unable to walk. His legs were paralyzed. It was then that doctors discovered a tumor on his spine. They performed surgery and sent him home with recommendations for physical therapy to help him get back his strength. After several months of physical therapy, Dad was still unable to walk and enduring a lot of pain.

The day after she received the bad news, Mom started making arrangements to move the family to Quincy, Illinois. She told Dad that they were going there so that he could have better medical care to hasten his recovery. Just before she had movers pack up the household, I flew with Dad to New Orleans, where he was admitted to the Ochsner

Clinic. I stayed with Aunt Genie and spent a few days wandering around New Orleans before having my afternoon visit with Dad in the clinic. I took a Greyhound bus back to college in Ohio just before Mom arrived from Mexico with Ruth and Eunice. They settled in Quincy, Illinois, with Dad being transferred to Blessing Hospital. The doctor in New Orleans had said it would be "too depressing" to tell Dad about his short life expectancy, so it was left for a doctor in Quincy to share the bad news a couple months later.

Mom said that Dad became depressed when he learned about his prognosis, but soon he was praying, "Thy will be done." I had really expected that his faith would see him through, so I was not surprised.

Dad continued to decline in the hospital, and he was given morphine to ease the pain. I was away at college, so I didn't see him, and my sisters, still in high school, did not visit him much near the end, because he was so weak and emaciated that they were uncomfortable being around him.

He died on November 8, 1964, at the age of fifty-six. The next day, I traveled from Wooster, Ohio, to Quincy, Illinois, with Will and his wife, Peg, and her parents. Seeing my father in a casket made me very sad but also brought back many memories for me of the fine, generous man who was my father.

Many years later, I jumped at the chance to become a hospice volunteer, wishing that my father's final months had been handled better and hoping to help other people have a more satisfactory end of life. I have now been working with hospice for a number of years, and I am happy with the good work we are able to do, helping patients live their final days in the comfort of their own home and making it possible for families to care for them.

CHAPTER 39

My Father's Legacy

THROUGHOUT HIS LIFE, DAD WAS constantly interested in learning. He had repeated eighth grade in the one-room country schoolhouse of his childhood because he thought that that was all the education that would be available to him. He then found a way to go to high school. After high school, he went to Wheaton College in Wheaton, Illinois, working part time to help with finances. Then he studied at Dallas Theological Seminary in Texas. Years later, he completed graduate work at Princeton Theological Seminary.

His thoughts on religion were constantly evolving. As far as I know, he never had serious doubts about Christianity, but he definitely questioned some beliefs. The first one I know about was premillennialism, which is the belief that Jesus will physically return to the earth before the millennium, a literal thousand-year golden age of peace. In the 1940s when he was a missionary with the Central American Mission, he began to question premillennialism, which was one of the beliefs required of their missionaries. When he realized that he could not accept that belief, he resigned from his missionary position and returned to the United States. That was how I happened to be born in the United States. Soon after that, he decided that he could accept premillennialism after all, and he returned to the mission field in Honduras, along with his wife and two children.

Once, when he heard my brother singing, "Give me that old time religion, it's good enough for me," I overheard Dad telling Will that sometimes old-time religion was not as good as it should be, and we needed to be open to new ideas.

He was an avid reader of Christian Century, a publication that "has informed and shaped progressive, mainline Christianity. As a voice of generous orthodoxy, the Century is both loyal to the church and open to the world." He also read books by Teilhard de Chardin, Paul Tillich, Dietrich Bonhoeffer, and many other influential Christian writers.

He usually came upstairs from his office around five in the evening and changed into old clothes. Then he often spent an hour sitting comfortably on a rattan chair, reading one of his deep philosophical books or publications and deeply pondering what he was reading. I could tell by his concentrated expression and his lack of reaction to whatever was happening around him that he was deep in thought. That lasted until Mom called us all to dinner right around six.

Then, after mealtime grace, Dad was ready to engage with each member of the family, doing what he could to get a general conversation going. We children talked about incidents at school, and often someone had a joke or story to share—my parents were both fond of the little humorous stories in Reader's Digest.

One of my father's favorite stories was about a city boy who goes to visit his friend in the country. The city boy looks at all the produce growing in the garden and says, "You certainly have a lot of food! What do you do with all of it?"

The country boy responds, "We eat what we can, and what we can't, we can" (by which he meant, preserve food in canning jars).

The city boy went home confused. He told his parents, "My friend told me that, with all the food they grew, they ate what they could, and what they couldn't they could."

He also once told us, after one of his trips around Central America, "One village where I stayed had really big mosquitoes. Many of them weigh a pound! And they sit on the trees and bark."

Dad was friendly and good-natured about meeting new people. He often greeted people he encountered and started conversations with strangers when he could. He seemed to be comfortable with a variety of people, including the black Jamaican men who washed cars by the bachelor quarters and the San Blas Indians he met, as well as some Panamanians.

Once when I read Screwtape Letters by C. S. Lewis, he looked at the passages that I had underlined and said, "The parts you have underlined are a good outline of fundamentalist Christianity. I used to think that, if I was not a fundamentalist, I was not really a Christian. But I don't think that way anymore. You know, people can change."

Whenever he had the opportunity, he enjoyed having deep theological discussions with other ministers and missionaries. We sometimes went on vacation to the beach with the family of our pastor, Ted Franklin. He and Dad would have deep discussions standing in the surf, while we children played in the water around them. Dad also took a box of books along when we went on vacation, and he spent many hours reading.

I am also an avid reader; sometimes I enjoy light fiction, but I am often attracted to serious books on various aspects of spirituality. I like to think I picked up that habit from him.

CHAPTER 40

Marriage

Wooster, Ohio, 1966

TERRY HAD ASSUMED THAT HE would delay marriage until he'd completed his education, which was several years in the future. I was eager to start living my dream of getting married and living happily ever after. Because I had finished college and had a job and we were in love, I saw no reason to wait much longer.

We were married the summer before his senior year of college. After we said our vows in the college chapel, in front of our families and friends, I burst into tears, overcome with emotion. The first part of my dream of getting married and living happily ever after was actually coming true! I was really married! I had a permanent, loving partner to share my life with. With my husband by my side, I would be better able to find my place in the adult world. And I would soon begin to enjoy the pleasures of sex that I had craved for so very long. Terry graciously pulled a clean white handkerchief from his pocket for me to wipe my tears.

I continued to work to support us through Terry's senior year. We had a modest but enjoyable life. I went to work while he went to classes; I learned how to prepare meals for two and how to shop and have on hand what we needed. We spent our evenings together at home, and occasionally we got together with friends. We enjoyed a lot of banter and conversation.

I enjoyed living in the same apartment with him, and we were glad for the freedom to have sex, although I didn't find it quite as thrilling as I had hoped.

CHAPTER 41

Joining the Lutheran Church

Bloomington, Indiana 1968

A YEAR AFTER TERRY AND I were married, we moved to Bloomington, Indiana, where he was enrolled in graduate school at Indiana University. We built our love nest with used furniture and a new Beautyrest mattress in a tenth-floor apartment. Except for the fact that I had a job to support us while he was a student, we imitated our parents' lives: I did the cooking and cleaning and grocery shopping and laundry, and he came home and ate dinner and then went back to his studies while I washed dishes in the kitchenette. I baked his favorite pies for him and packed his lunch. And we went to church on Sundays.

After visiting several churches, we were enthusiastic about joining the vibrant congregation of a Missouri Synod Lutheran Church. Terry had grown up in a Lutheran church, and I found it refreshingly different from the church of my childhood. We both enjoyed the activities of a group of friendly young couples—frequent get-togethers in homes, progressive dinners, and many good conversations.

In college, I had continued to attend church regularly, as was my habit. I enjoyed the wonderful organ and choir music at the college chapel, and Rev. Asbury, the college chaplain, gave thought-provoking sermons that enlarged my view of Christianity. I also took courses in Old Testament and New Testament. And by the time I graduated, I felt comfortably settled into my life as a young adult Christian.

When Terry and I decided to formally join the church, I was required to take catechism classes because I did not have a Lutheran background. Pastor Ken led the small group of candidates through the basic teachings of the church, and it all sounded very familiar to me. So it was with a sense of comfort and pleasant anticipation that I approached the brief ceremony of becoming a member of the Lutheran Church.

Just before the ceremony, Pastor Ken rehearsed our vows with us. He said, "This is what you will say: 'I believe in God the Father. I believe in Jesus Christ, his son, who died for our sins and was resurrected in glory. I believe in the Holy Spirit. And I believe that the Missouri Synod Lutheran Church is the only true church.'"

"I can't say that!" I protested vehemently.

Pastor Ken responded, "You don't have to believe it. Just say it."

What should I do? I had to decide quickly. It had never occurred to me that one denomination of Protestant Christians would consider themselves to be "the only true church." I knew that different denominations had their own beliefs and practices, but I thought they also respected other Christians with different habits. I didn't want to say something I didn't believe. But on the other hand, I didn't want to make waves or cause trouble. I also had a strong desire to be a fully accepted member of this church.

So I went against my better judgment. I said, "I believe that the Missouri Synod Lutheran Church is the only true church." But I didn't believe it, and I certainly did not feel good about saying it.

Afterward, when I told Terry about it, he exclaimed, "He told you to lie? Incredible! My dear lying wife." And he kissed me affectionately. Then he said, "Well, anyway, now you're a Lutheran, believe it or not!"

That event set me off again—with questions that had begun years earlier. Do Christians believe what they say they believe? Do differences between denominations really matter? What is the actual truth about Christianity? Is Christianity better than any other religion?

Once started, the questions kept quietly fermenting in my mind and heart. I didn't share many of my thoughts with my husband. I was in the habit of keeping these thoughts private. And I had the sense that he had little interest in these questions that were so vital to me. As a result, a rift was beginning to grow between us was that was one of many factors leading to the end of our marriage fifteen years later.

CHAPTER 42

A Big Decision

Fort Leonard Wood, Missouri, 1969

IN 1968, AFTER TERRY'S FIRST year of graduate school, he was one of many young men to receive a draft notice, due to the Vietnam War. So we packed up and left Bloomington, Indiana. After basic training, when Terry was stationed at Ft. Leonard Wood, Missouri, I joined him there, and we continued our married life in a small mobile home a few miles from the base. I taught piano lessons to children of army officers and spent evenings and weekends with my soldier husband until he went to Vietnam.

After Terry left, my life changed. For the first time ever, I was alone, without parents or teachers or husband to tell me what to do. I spent my days doing yoga, watching soap operas, teaching piano lessons, and visiting with friends. I tried alcoholic beverages for the first time in my life. And, not incidentally, I discovered I was pregnant a few weeks after Terry left.

I read the books I wanted to read. I read Herman Hesse's Siddhartha, which introduced me to Eastern spirituality. I read Everything You Always Wanted to Know about Sex (But Were Afraid to Ask) and realized that Terry and I had a lot to learn. I read The Feminine Mystique by Betty Friedan and started thinking about my life as a person, not just as a wife.

Although I had indulged in my own secret thoughts ever since early childhood, I had always lived with people who tended to oppose those thoughts in one way or another. I often felt like the children of the English mother who said to the nanny, "Go into the garden and see what the children are doing and tell them not to." Suddenly, I had the freedom to think what I wanted to think with nobody around to tell me otherwise.

I had always understood Christianity to be a religion of beliefs. "Believe in the Lord Jesus Christ, and you will be saved" (Acts 16:31). I had struggled mightily to believe in God, to believe that Jesus was the only-begotten Son of God (if we are all children of God, then how could God have an only-begotten Son?). And I had constantly struggled to try to believe in Jesus Christ without having serious doubts. After Pastor Ken had told me to say that I believe that the Missouri Synod Lutheran Church was the only true church, even though he knew that I didn't believe it, I began to wonder how many Christians said they believed, or pretended to believe, things they didn't really believe. How much of religion was based on false premises? And how could so many people really and truly believe what, to me, was so very difficult to believe? I was now alone with my own thoughts, with nobody trying to talk me out of them, and I decided that I did not want to consider myself a Christian anymore. I felt a great sense of relief.

In a letter to Terry I wrote, "After giving it a lot of thought, I have decided I don't want to call myself a Christian anymore. Especially after Pastor Ken told me to say what I don't believe, I have realized that many Christians don't believe what they say they believe. So what is the point of pretending to be a Christian?"

Terry responded, "That's okay with me. Church never meant much to me anyway."

I thus became unmoored from the spiritual anchor that had been the foundation of my life—and of the lives of my parents and grandparents and probably of many generations of my family before them. I was drifting alone in an unknown sea, not knowing what I might find to grab onto. But it felt much better than continuing to adhere to a religion that I didn't really believe.

I felt greatly relieved that I no longer had to try to make sense of the contradictions in the Bible. I felt no obligation to even read or think about the Bible! Not considering myself a Christian freed me from having to define myself as one kind of Christian or another, with all its permutations that had never made sense to me. Among those were infant baptism versus adult baptism; literal versus liberal interpretation of the Bible; and all the rules that some Christian groups enforced and about which some were very strict, such as no drinking, no dancing, no makeup for women, and other restrictions.

All the attitudes regarding women that came from the Bible did not have to affect me anymore, which was a good thing because I was getting caught up in a new wave of feminism.

I also felt no obligation to think about God or to pray. Without the constant reminders from the Bible, I didn't have to think about Big, Bad, Mean, Scary God as I had in my childhood when I was exposed to daily Bible reading. This was a great relief! I was dimly aware that I wanted something, but I didn't know where to find it. And I was quite sure I was not going to find it in Christianity.

Of course, a lifetime of rigorous indoctrination was not going to disappear all at once. But at least I was beginning to break free.

And I had fulfilled my wish to get married and live happily ever after. Well, at least I had gotten married. And we had been happy. (This would change after our year of separation due to his deployment to Vietnam, but I didn't know that yet.)

However, I was still associated with the church by virtue of playing the organ for many religious services. Even today, while I am definitely not a Christian, I am still employed as a church organist and enjoy the fellowship of the church. And I appreciate being together with people who have gathered to worship God. I give myself the freedom to refrain from saying the prayers or creeds, and I accept the teachings that are useful for me and quietly reject the rest.

I didn't tell my mother that I had broken away from the church. She had always followed, unquestioningly, the teachings of the church, first as interpreted by her preacher father and then as interpreted by her preacher husband. I was sure that she would not understand my decision and would try to talk me into becoming a Christian again. I often think that the one person who might have been able to convince me to remain a Christian was my father. He was as devout and sincere and enthusiastic about his faith as anyone I have ever known, and he knew me and loved me and generally understood me. However, he had died five years before I made that decision.

CHAPTER 43

Mountain Climbing

FROM EARLIEST CHILDHOOD, MY MOTHER told me that I must never, ever touch myself "down there." So I didn't, at least not until adolescence. But as a child I wondered why my parents didn't seem interested in delightful feelings "down there" and why boys were different from girls. And how did a baby get into a woman's stomach anyway? And how did it get out? I had plenty of curiosity. But in the 1950s, it wasn't easy to get answers. Finally in sixth grade, my teacher made sure that all her students learned the "facts of life."

Before Terry and I were married, I was eagerly anticipating the physical side of marriage. After I married him in 1966 at age twenty-one, I was disappointed that, on our excursions, he quickly scrambled up the mountain peak, while I was still strolling through the foothills, if you know what I mean. Foothills are pleasurable in their own way, but I wanted to get to the top. I kept thinking that would just happen naturally, with time and patience—if I would just relax, if I kept my concentration and focus better. Maybe faking it would help. And if I were really normal, it would just happen, wouldn't it? There was even a scriptural basis for my attitude: In I Corinthians 13, St. Paul says, "Love bears all things, believes all things, hopes all things, endures all things." So I kept on believing and hoping and enduring.

In 1969, Terry was sent to Vietnam for a year. While he was away, I had plenty of opportunity for solo mountain climbing expeditions, so I knew it was possible for me to reach the summit; I was just a slow hiker. I was also getting ideas from my new book Everything You Always Wanted to Know about Sex.

When we got back together, my husband read the book, and we were finally able to talk about it. But we still didn't know what to do. We couldn't seem to change our habits that had him jumping off the mountain before I had a chance to get halfway up. Eventually I took my problem to a therapist. She helped me release some of the anxiety and frustration that had been building, she helped me learn how to ask for what I wanted, and she helped my husband learn how to satisfy me. We discovered that, even if he had already bounded off the mountain, he could still lead me to the top, with a little care and willingness. Although it was not as "natural" or romantic as I might have wished, I had the satisfaction of experiencing the view from the top with him. I finally felt happy and fulfilled.

CHAPTER 44

Thailand

Thailand, 1972–1974

WHEN TERRY RETURNED FROM VIETNAM, our lives were very different from what they had been before he went away. During our year of separation he had discovered Asian music, as he had taken advantage of many cultural opportunities, going to concerts in Saigon as often as he could. He was so fascinated with Asian music that he was determined to return to Indiana University to study ethnomusicology. I was trying to find my own identity and was no longer the compliant little wife I had been before. We also had a child—Sonia had been born during that year and was five months old when her father returned. And we didn't go to church.

After completing most of his graduate studies, Terry was fortunate to be accepted for a Ford Foundation grant to study the music of northeast Thailand. So we put our possessions in storage and headed off to Thailand, with three-year-old Sonia and a few suitcases of warm-weather clothing.

We stayed in Bangkok for two months of language training. I saw many beautiful Buddhist temples while we were there. We saw small Buddhas, huge Buddhas, standing Buddhas, reclining Buddhas, and seated Buddhas. Sonia learned to sit like Buddha. We saw orange-robed Buddhist monks going from door to door with their begging bowls, collecting food for their daily meal. We saw adolescent novice monks. Terry and I called them monklets. I heard chanting of Buddhist prayers, and I saw performances of Thai shadow puppet theater, complete with exotic singing and instrumental music, acting out scenes from the Ramakian, the Thai version of the Hindu Ramayana. We were especially fascinated by Hanuman, the monkey god. All of it struck me as interesting and exotic; however, I did not find in it the spiritual inspiration I was seeking.

When we moved to northeast Thailand, where Terry was to do his year of research, we had more exposure to Thai Buddhism. During our very first night there, we were awakened at 4:00 a.m. by enormously loud speaker systems blaring Buddhist chants and prayers at a temple close to our house. It was for a festival that continued for three days of deafening sound from 4:00 a.m. until 9:00 p.m.

I noticed other fascinating aspects of Thai beliefs. Almost every house had a "spirit house" mounted on a pole, usually about ten feet from the house. The spirit houses were small, approximately one foot in each dimension, and some of them were quite ornate. Their purpose was to give spirits, or ghosts, somewhere to live so they wouldn't bother people. There were often small offerings of food or flowers placed at the door of the spirit house in memory of deceased relatives.

Thai Buddhists sought ways to make merit for themselves. They apparently believed that merit accumulated in their lifetime would help them secure a better place in heaven. Giving food to monks was one merit-making activity, and making donations to the local temple was another. If one was serious about it, one could have a special merit-making ceremony. In the Thai language this was called a Tamboon.

A few months before we were due to leave Thailand, our landlord and landlady asked us if they could have a Tamboon in our house, which was larger than their house next door. We agreed, and they went to work to prepare for it. This involved cooking large amounts of food, bringing in flowers and other decorations, putting down straw mats for people to sit on, and providing spittoons for the monks. Many adults in northeast Thailand were in the habit of chewing betel nut, which necessitated spitting out the red juice periodically. The spittoons put in place for the monks ensured that they would be able to remain sitting during their prayers and chanting without having to get up to spit.

On the morning of the Tamboon, ten orange-robed monks were ushered into our house and seated on the mats beside the colorfully decorated spittoons. Then the house filled with friends and neighbors of our landlord. The monks chanted prayers and scriptures for about an hour. I did not understand anything that was being said, as my rudimentary understanding of the Thai language did not include religious terms. When they were finished chanting, the monks were ceremoniously served the best food. When they were satisfied, everyone else ate.

The food included huge mounds of sticky rice, with bowls of pungent sauce for dipping handfuls of rice. There was salad called som tum made of finely chopped green papaya mixed with fish sauce, hot chilies, and lime juice. And chopped beef and barbecued chicken were served. There was plenty for everyone, and our landlord and his wife were happy that they had lived long enough to have a successful Tamboon.

On our way home from Thailand, we stopped in Nepal for a few days of sightseeing and then spent one day in India on our way to Israel and Switzerland. In a small bookshop in New Delhi, I bought a copy of Autobiography of a Yogi by Paramahansa Yogananda. I was attracted to the title, as I had been interested in yoga for a few years. I was mesmerized by the beautiful picture of Yogananda on the cover, with his long wavy black hair and his calm face with deep love radiating from his soft eyes. I was delighted to learn that he had been a highly evolved spiritual leader and had lived in America in my lifetime (he died in 1952), and I could find out about him through this book that he had written. Probably there were people still alive who had known him personally. As I began to read, I knew I had found a treasure, one that would help to guide and inspire me on my journey.

I had wondered, for a long time, why God had inspired the writers of the Bible and then apparently never inspired anyone in a similar way for two thousand years. If God spoke to the writers of the Bible, why didn't God continue speaking in more recent times? I had been wishing, without really knowing what I was wishing, for a living spiritual master who would be accessible to guide people as they are today and who could do it without being weighed down by centuries of Christian dogma and tradition. Although Yogananda was no longer alive on earth, the fact that he had recently been here gave me hope that it might be possible for me to find the kind of spiritual guide that I craved.

CHAPTER 45

My Daughters

BEFORE SONIA WAS BORN, I made several decisions. I was determined that I would not take her anywhere between the ages of six months and three years, as I had seen a lot of unhappy parents with their fussy infants and uncomfortable toddlers. I also decided that I would let my children eat the amount that was right for them and not try to coerce them to eat more. I had been quite a picky eater as a child, and my parents often tried to get me to eat "just a little bit more."

When I was being discharged from the army hospital with my new baby, I was amazed that they just let me take her home, even though I had given little evidence that I knew how to take care of a baby. When I was young, I thought that my parents knew everything and that they were completely confident in their parenting skills. I even fantasized that parents, and maybe teachers too, went to meetings where they learned the common phrases used by parents and teachers, such as, "As I was saying before I was so rudely interrupted," and, "Money doesn't grow on trees," and, "There are starving people in Africa who would gladly eat your dinner," and "Stop crying, or I'll give you something to really cry about." I realized that I was deficient in parenting skills and probably was not going to gain knowledge very quickly, so I thought of myself less like a mother and more like a big sister—one who was helpful and affectionate but sometimes didn't really know what she was doing.

Sonia was five years old when Esther was born. A few days after the new baby arrived, Sonia announced, "When the baby grows up to be a child, I'm going to play with her."

That was what she did as soon as Esther was ready to engage in activities with her.

I wanted my children to be as independent as possible. I sent them outside to play, and they made up their own games while I kept an eye on them from the kitchen. When they were old enough, I allowed them to play in a field a couple of blocks away from our house. When Esther was quite young, she liked to climb a small tree by our house, sometimes looking into the second-floor window. I knew that she was not reckless and always found safe ways to enjoy her adventures, so I tried not to limit her actions. Although I was afraid to look at her when she was climbing a tree, I still encouraged her to do it.

They spent many hours playing "school." Sonia was the teacher, and Esther, starting around the age of three, was the student. Without any help, Sonia prepared lessons in reading and math that were usually perfectly geared to the needs of her student, and Esther happily absorbed the lessons. To this day, Sonia still enjoys teaching and Esther still enjoys learning.

I encouraged them to entertain themselves, although I was willing to play with them when it seemed appropriate. One activity that we all enjoyed together was reading books. Every week we brought home a stack of books from the library, and I enjoyed the stories and pictures as much as they did. I have fond memories of sitting between two freshly bathed little girls, reading them their bedtime stories.

I am grateful that I still enjoy a fond relationship with both my daughters, and they also stay happily in touch with each other, even though we all are separated geographically.

Reading to Sonia and Esther

CHAPTER 46

Unity

Ohio, 1977–1983

IN MY SEARCH FOR AN alternative to the Christian religion that I had turned away from, I was attracted to Unity Church. I was living in Kent, Ohio, with my professor husband and our two young daughters when I learned about Unity. The nearest Unity Church was in Akron, about fifteen miles away. I went there and liked it, so I started taking my daughters with me on Sunday mornings. Terry preferred to stay at home in his book-lined study, reading about ethnomusicology and preparing lectures for his classes.

Founded by Charles and Myrtle Fillmore in 1889, Unity Church and Unity School of Christianity have a very tolerant and open-minded attitude toward the Bible and other scriptures of the world. The Fillmores were influenced by Emma Curtis Hopkins, E. B. Weeks, and others. In 1887 Myrtle Fillmore, suffering from tuberculosis, went to a lecture by E. B. Weeks, and came out with an affirmation that helped to restore her to health. She repeated, over and over, "I am a child of God, and therefore, I do not inherit sickness." She and her husband started Unity School of Christianity near Kansas City and began publishing a magazine in 1889. Unity Church grew out of that, even though they had no intention of starting a church.

I enjoyed meeting a diverse group of friendly people at Unity. The minister or one of the frequent guest speakers usually read from the Bible, but they also included wisdom from other traditions in their talks, and even their interpretations of the Bible felt very generous and open to me. Hymns were accompanied on an electronic organ, and we always ended the service by holding hands and singing "Let There Be Peace on Earth, and Let It Begin with Me," a song I still love.

The church had Sunday school classes for children. After Sonia started attending the class for seven-year-olds, I asked her how she liked it. She told me it was boring. I had heard that they were looking for a teacher for her class (an elderly man had been teaching it until they could find a regular teacher), so I asked her if she would like it better if I taught it. She brightened up and said yes enthusiastically. So I volunteered and started teaching her class.

After I had been teaching for a couple of weeks, one Sunday I was ready to go out the door with my daughters. I had two-year-old Esther with me, but I couldn't find Sonia. It was a chilly day, so I was quite sure she was in the house. I searched everywhere, calling her name. Finally after half an hour of searching, I found her carefully hidden in a small space behind her father's desk. It then dawned on me that maybe she really didn't want to go to Unity.

I said, "Sonia, you really don't want to go with me, do you?"

She said, "I don't want to go because I don't believe in God."

She was relieved that I got the message. So she stayed home with her Dad. Esther went with me and stayed in the nursery with other toddlers, and I continued to teach the seven-year-old Sunday school class.

Years later, Sonia told me why she had become an atheist. When she was five years old, she wanted to believe in God, so she lay in bed and tried to believe in God. She tried for several days, but she just couldn't believe in God, so she decided that God didn't exist.

Interestingly, after she started having her own children, she wanted a church community for her family. She even asked me for advice! Since her husband had come from a Thai Buddhist family (although they were not very much involved with that religion), I suggested that they might find a Buddhist group. Another possibility was the Unitarian church. They started going to the Unitarian Church, and at first, she liked it a lot. She called me to say, "Mommy, it was great! They didn't even mention God!"

CHAPTER 47

Changing My Diet

A YEAR AFTER GRADUATING FROM COLLEGE, I found employment at Apple Creek State Hospital in Apple Creek, Ohio, working as a music therapist with the intellectually challenged residents. At lunchtime, I brought my brown bag lunch to the table with six other women who also worked there. One of the women, Esther Eyman, was a vigorous woman in her seventies, who energetically oversaw the volunteer program at the hospital. She ate cheese and lettuce sandwiches on dark heavy bread, and she was fond of telling us that she ate organically grown food whenever possible. She also took supplements, and she attributed her good health and energy to the foods and vitamins she consumed.

As her health had been quite poor before she changed her diet, I became inspired to try organic foods and supplements myself. This was during the late 1960s, when few people were paying attention to the connection between diet and health, and little was being said about chemicals used in agriculture. Rachel Carson's landmark book, Silent Spring, had been published in 1962, and people were very gradually getting used to the idea that environmental poisons might be harmful.

I started buying brown bread and brown rice instead of white; I added more fresh fruits and vegetables to our diet, along with yogurt. I read Adelle Davis's books about health foods and supplements, and I started taking several supplements to improve my health, which was already reasonably good.

A year or so later, I started getting interested in yoga. Yoga classes were rare and hard to find, but I bought a few books to guide my yoga practice. Both my sister Ruth and I are convinced that yoga practice aided us in being able to conceive our first children. Along with the yoga postures, I noticed that writers of the yoga books recommended a vegetarian diet. For several years, I wanted to experience becoming a vegetarian, but I put it off—first, because I was pregnant and then nursing a baby, and I didn't want to make drastic changes. Then, when it became clear that we would be going to Thailand for fourteen months, I decided to wait with my vegetarian experiment until I would be able to have more control over my environment. After returning from Thailand, we lived with Terry's parents for a year, and that also did not seem like a good time to add extra complications to mealtimes.

After Terry and I were settled into our own home with our two young daughters, I decided it was finally time for me to become a vegetarian. Terry was not interested in changing his diet, so I cooked vegetarian meals for myself, with a side of meat for those who wanted it. We had navy bean soup with chopped ham that could be added. We had meatless lasagna that needed no additions. We had potato soup with tuna salad on the side. This worked reasonably well for the family.

When we went to visit my mother, she could not understand why I didn't eat meat. She would say, "A little meat won't hurt you." I think she believed that it was unbiblical, even unchristian not to eat meat. After all, she had never been to a church dinner where meat was not served. And the Bible was full of meat eaters. The only exceptions I can think of were Daniel and his buddies. Before they were thrown into the lion's den, they were living in the king's palace and were offered the meat and wine similar to that served to the king. They declined, asking for beans and water.

Other than that, apparently all the characters of the Bible were eaters of meat, including Jesus and his disciples, who at least ate fish. In fact, Genesis hints that God prefers meat to vegetables. When Cain and Abel offered their sacrifices to God, Cain brought his produce, and Abel brought his animals. When God showed respect to Abel's offering of meat but not to Cain's offering of vegetables, Cain killed his brother in a fit of jealous rage. God continued to request burnt offerings of animal flesh. Even when Abraham was about to obediently sacrifice his son to the Lord, what was given to him in place of his son was a ram. For their Passover meal, the Israelites were commanded to slaughter and eat a choice lamb. When the prodigal son returned home after a long absence, in a story told by Jesus, his father ordered the fatted calf to be killed for a meal of celebration.

Because my mother constantly referred to the Bible as her main source of inspiration and guidance, she considered that my vegetarian diet was not only strange but also suspiciously unchristian. She wasn't interested in my reasons for becoming a vegetarian. I wanted to feel lighter and clearer; I was hoping that following a vegetarian diet would help my efforts at meditation. In addition, I was hoping that it would help to reduce my sex drive. (In case you're wondering, it did not make a difference.)

After three and a half years of not eating meat, I decided to return to a full diet, including meat. By getting very gradually onto meat, I was able to make a smooth transition.

Looking back, I see my first vegetarian phase as an important step in asserting myself as a person, instead of catering to my husband or my mother as I had previously been in the habit of doing.

CHAPTER 48

Teaching Piano Lessons

MAJORING IN MUSIC AT THE College of Wooster, I took piano lessons during every semester, played in recitals frequently, played a concerto with an orchestra, and presented full-length solo recitals during my junior and senior years. I also took courses in music theory, music history, and orchestration. I learned how trends in music interacted with trends in art and architecture and literature, as well as with political events. And I had one course in piano pedagogy, where I learned a few things about teaching piano lessons.

While still in college, I taught a few students—a couple of adults, a few children, and one teenager. I enjoyed working with them to help them develop their ability to read and play music, and, at first, I taught in a manner similar to the way I had been taught.

As I moved on in my life, I continued to teach at least a few piano students, because there was a demand for it, and I enjoyed teaching. In fact, the only year I didn't teach at all was the year we were in Thailand. Where we lived, in a small town in northeast Thailand, there were no pianos or keyboard instruments available. I missed playing the piano, and I missed teaching during that year.

Back in the United States, I found a few students to teach—organ as well as piano. I wanted to try group piano teaching, so I bought two upright Kawai pianos—lovely instruments with good tone—and set about to teach two or more students together. This seemed like a really good idea. I could charge each student less than the fee for private lessons, but I would earn more money per hour of teaching. Students would have the pleasure of playing together, and as I taught new ideas and new music, the students would help each other learn. It would be fun! Students would learn well!

However, I had difficulty keeping students' attention. Some learned quickly and were ready to move on, while others needed more time to master the pieces they were playing. I soon gave up and went back to teaching individual lessons.

When my children were young, I had my piano studio in the basement, and they had the run of the rest of the house. However, when Esther was two or three years old, she would open the basement door and come crying to me. So I hired a neighboring teenager to watch the children while I was teaching. Because I usually taught students in the afternoon after school, I often made preparations for dinner ahead of time so that we could eat soon after I finished teaching.

When I heard about the Suzuki approach to music, I wanted to learn more about it. Mr. Shinichi Suzuki was a Japanese violinist and educator. He observed that all babies learn to talk. Nobody asks if they are gifted with language; people just assume that a child will learn to imitate the language that he hears people speaking. Mr. Suzuki decided to use the same approach with learning music. Students as young as three years old would listen to recordings of the music they were going to play, and when they started to play it themselves, they already knew exactly how it was supposed to sound.

The Suzuki approach was adapted for piano in the 1970s, and soon after that, I began using it in my teaching. Several of my students got along very well listening to music and then playing what they heard. This is sometimes called "playing by ear." However, when I introduced them to reading music several months later, they were resistant to playing simple songs by reading music when they could already play more complicated music just by hearing it.

I knew that being able to read music was essential for their musical development, so I developed my own hybrid approach. I taught them to read music and play simple pieces by reading at the same time that they were learning their first Suzuki pieces by listening to them. I was happy with this approach for several years. Students enjoyed playing both the music they heard and the music they read.

I let go of the Suzuki approach a few years ago and started focusing on whatever music was most meaningful to each student. I did this because I realized that the most important key to learning is enthusiasm. When students really enjoy the music they are playing, they tend to practice more and accomplish far more than they do when playing music they don't like. When I sense that a student is not enjoying a piece, I often ask him or her, "Do you want to keep playing this?"

If the student says no, we move on to something that he or she can enjoy better.

I am fond of saying, "There is so much good music in the world; we should not waste our time playing music we don't like."

Fortunately, music publishers have made my job much easier in the last twenty or thirty years by publishing simple but attractive arrangements of popular songs, Disney movie themes, jazz and blues, hymns, songs that young children sing, themes from classical music, and so on. In fact, there are several series of that type arranged for progressively advancing students, so I have the pleasure of presenting students with a choice of different types of music at their level. I usually use at least one supplementary book along with their standard piano instruction books.

In addition, I sometimes prepare my own arrangement of a song that is especially meaningful to a student. I use Finale, a music-writing program, on my computer. Sometimes it's as easy as taking a simple tune and adding an accompaniment within the student's capability. Occasionally I have listened repeatedly to a popular song, if haven't been able to find a written version. I listen and transcribe it to make an arrangement that will be accessible for the student. For example, I created an easy arrangement of the chorus of "Cielito Lindo," the theme song for a Mexican soccer team, for a boy who is a huge fan of the team. I also tried to humor a teenage girl by arranging a song called "Art Is Dead," including profanities, to try to encourage her interest. It may have helped a little.

There have been times in the past when I did not think very highly of my piano teaching. I thought I should get into a "real career"—that teaching piano was just something I knew how to do but it wasn't very important. Now I see it as a wonderful way to connect with people and a way that I can assist individuals to develop their own musical skills and enjoy the pleasures and satisfaction of playing the piano.

CHAPTER 49

Yoga

AROUND 1968, I READ AN article in a woman's magazine describing some basic yoga postures and suggesting that, in addition to other benefits, they might be helpful in improving and regulating a woman's reproductive system. I definitely wanted to be healthy. I had started eating "health foods" and taking supplements a year or two before that, and I was also hoping to get pregnant. My menstrual periods were rather irregular, and I wanted to tone up my system the best way I could.

I started practicing yoga postures, first with the suggestions from the magazine, and then with the aid of a book on yoga by Indra Devi, who was hugely influential in introducing yoga to the United States. There were no yoga teachers available where I lived, so I relied entirely on the magazine and the book. I discovered that the postures I tried helped me to feel good physically and emotionally, so I made them part of my daily routine.

Once when Terry and I were visiting my mother, while I was practicing my yoga routine, I heard my mother ask my husband, suspiciously, "Is that some kind of religion she is practicing?"

Terry did not share my enthusiasm for yoga, but he tried to be supportive, and he assured my mother that it did not conflict with any religious principles.

I'm not sure that yoga had anything to do with it, but a few months after I started my practice, I got pregnant. I didn't realize I was pregnant until after Terry left for Vietnam, where the army ordered him to go for a year. Thus, I was left in Missouri by myself to have my first baby without my husband present.

A year or two later, my sister Ruth was wanting to get pregnant, and I shared with her some of the yoga postures that I believed were helpful in toning up my reproductive system. She started doing them, and she got pregnant. There may or may not have been a connection between yoga and pregnancy, but we both had a sense that practicing yoga was good for us.

I continued a daily practice of yoga postures for several years. When Sonia was very young, I had a habit of getting up very early to practice yoga, because I knew that I would have little peace and solitude after she got up. Eventually, she was sometimes able to entertain herself for a few minutes while I was doing some of my postures. Once when I was lying on my stomach holding on to my ankles with my knees bent, she remarked, "Mommy backwards!" She sometimes joined me in some of the easier postures.

Eventually I found some yoga classes, and I enjoyed going to them, practicing yoga with other people, and learning to improve the way I did my practice.

Now, many years later, I have other forms of exercise and body maintenance that I like, and I still practice some yoga postures on occasion. I am glad that yoga has become popular and quite mainstream.

CHAPTER 50

Going to Georgia

AFTER READING YOGANANDA'S AUTOBIOGRAPHY I began studying a correspondence course that he had written. The lessons in the course included instructions for meditation. I carefully followed the lessons, and I was beginning to meditate shortly before Esther was born. I expected that, after her birth, I would be able to meditate while she was sleeping. However, she was a very fussy baby, and I rarely had more than a few minutes of peace. So I gave up.

A few years later, I decided to try meditating again. This time, it was not a crying baby but my own overactive mind that interfered. I gave up after a few attempts.

However, I still wanted to know more about Yogananda and his teachings. I became very interested when I learned about Roy Eugene Davis. He had worked with Yogananda and had been part of Yogananda's organization for a number of years and then had founded his own spirituality center in Georgia. I did not think that Roy Eugene Davis was the same caliber of spiritual leader as Yogananda, but I believed and fervently hoped that he could help me in my spiritual search. I wrote to his organization in Georgia for more information.

I was thrilled when I received a small brochure describing his organization, called Center for Spiritual Awareness, and the programs offered there. However, my husband, Terry, was less enthusiastic. When he saw the brochure that had arrived in the mail (we received very little mail in 1976), he said, "What is this fly-by-night organization? Look how cheaply printed this is! Who would be attracted to this? And why are they sending it to us?"

I tried to explain that I was interested in meditation and that Roy Eugene Davis had been a follower of Yogananda, who I greatly admired. Terry was not impressed.

A few weeks later, I signed up for a summer program at Center for Spiritual Awareness, choosing a time when Terry was planning to be on a trip with his father. My confirmation for the program arrived in the mail before I had gotten up the courage to tell Terry about it. He was not happy and tried to dissuade me from going, but I was determined.

When the time came, I drove from Ohio to Lakemont, Georgia, starting around 10:00 at night so that Sonia, and especially little Esther, would sleep during most of the trip. I had reserved a room in a motel near the center. And I had found a way to finance the trip, including registration fee, motel, meals, and childcare, as well as car expenses.

Two years later, I went to another summer program at Center for Spiritual Awareness during a time that Terry was away for the whole summer doing music research. This time, the girls and I planned to camp at a nearby state forest in Georgia. Just before we got to Knoxville, Tennessee, I noticed that, suddenly, the car had no braking power.

We spent a day hanging out at a repair shop, first getting the car fixed and then waiting for money to be wired from my bank in Ohio. This left us short of money for the rest of the summer, but I was still very happy to be able to go to the seminar.

Even though it rained every day, we still had a good experience camping, and I was even able to prepare meals over a little fire. I immersed myself in the study of meditation and spirituality, while my daughters participated in a program offered for children. Little by little, I was growing in a spiritual direction that felt good to me, and I was beginning to assert myself to get what I wanted.

CHAPTER 51

Matthew

DURING MY MARRIAGE WITH TERRY, I often felt attracted to other men. When we were in Thailand, there was Jack in our Thai language class and Prasert, a friendly young Thai man. I didn't exactly flirt with them, but I noticed a rush of pleasure when I was around them. Back in the United States there was Jim, a college friend of ours whose wife I also liked. One day when Terry and I were taking a walk, I said, "Even though I'm married to you, sometimes I feel attracted to other men."

He responded, "You are supposed to be attracted to only me, so you need to try harder not to be attracted to other men."

When we moved to our new home in Kent, Ohio, after Terry started teaching at Kent State University, I decided that I would limit my contacts to women and children. With two little kids at home, I could have a happy social life with mothers of other children. And I would teach a few piano students. This would be a simple solution to my problem!

Soon after fall semester began, Terry offered to post a notice on the bulletin board in the music department offering my services as an accompanist. Very soon, I had a phone call from Matthew, who was preparing to play his master's level violin recital. A few days later, he came to our house with his violin. I was immediately smitten by the shy, intense Japanese American violin student.

We rehearsed frequently over the next several months. I eagerly anticipated our times together, and I put great energy into practicing the piano parts. The high point of our program was the sonata for violin and piano by the Belgian French composer, Cesar Franck, a piece of lush romantic music that fed into my passion. I thought about Matthew constantly, although I never told him. Neither did I tell Terry how attracted I was to Matthew.

I was thrilled with our performance at the recital. I had started out feeling nervous and then somehow found a way to change the nervousness to excitement, with the result that I played better than ever, and we made beautiful music together. Terry, in the audience, clapped and cheered enthusiastically.

However, with no more rehearsals, our times together were over. Matthew finished his degree and went back to California. I was left with my memories and a growing realization that I was dissatisfied in my marriage.

Terry was completely caught up in being a professor of ethnomusicology, and he mostly ignored me and my interests, including my spiritual search. I also did not share his avid interest in ethnomusicology, although I tried to have some awareness of what he was doing. He paid little attention to our daughters, leaving me to do most of the parenting.

Over the next few years, I tried to revive our marriage. We went on date nights regularly. We studied Systematic Training for Effective Parenting and discovered that the principles of effective communication helped in our conversations with each other, even when we knew what "gimmick" the other was using. We went to a marriage counselor. We went together a few times; I continued going by myself when he stopped going.

As time went on, I felt lonelier when I was with him than when I was alone. I eventually knew that, for my own well-being, I had to get out.

CHAPTER 52

Divorce

Kent, Ohio, to Asheville, North Carolina, and back to Ohio, 1983–1988

I DID NOT WANT TO BE a divorced woman, but I felt like a big part of me was dying in the marriage. There were times I thought I should just tough it out for the sake of the children. However, I eventually decided that it was better for my daughters to have a mother who took care of herself than to have parents who stayed together physically but were emotionally distant. So the girls and I moved out at the end of the summer just before Terry came back from a summer of research in Taiwan. The changes required big adjustments, and we all had some challenging times.

Sonia was in junior high and had to go to a new school where she had no friends. She was very unhappy at school, and when she came home, the first thing she wanted to do was watch General Hospital, a TV soap opera. I watched it with her so that we had something to share and something to talk about. She enjoyed her guinea pigs, and liked to pretend they were miniature horses, so she made jumping hurdles for them out of tinker toys. She also took riding lessons, and when she learned about the possibility of renting a horse for the summer, she stubbornly went without lunch every day so she could save money for the horse. She spent much of the summer at the riding stable. A few months later, watching the winter Olympics on TV, she fell in love with ice-skating. We were able to get her to ice-skating lessons, and that has continued to be her passion.

Esther, meanwhile, was showing her strength as an excellent student. She was so utterly bored at the beginning of second grade that I prevailed upon the school principal to have her advanced to third grade. He reluctantly agreed to try it. Within a few days, she had caught up with her class, and she has continued to be an outstanding student all the way through postdoctoral studies.

Meanwhile, I was trying different jobs and starting to date but feeling rather aimless. After I learned about the Option Process, a way of working through personal issues by asking nonjudgmental questions, I spent two months at the Option Institute in Massachusetts, where I met Fred. The following year, we got married and moved to Asheville, North Carolina. I had great hopes that we would be able to handle any issues that came up in our relationship by using the Option Process. But in less than two years, our relationship had become intolerable for me.

At that time, I was the organist at a Methodist church, and I had a full schedule of piano students. Jim, who lived across from the church and sometimes sang bass in the choir, also had a significant background in playing the organ. He started coaching me and giving me useful tips on organ playing. Eventually I moved into the large Victorian house where he lived with his wife, June, and we had some very good times and also some very uncomfortable times together.

Meanwhile, Sonia and Esther had gone back to Ohio to live with their father. I didn't like being so far from them and seeing them only once or twice a year, so eventually I moved back to Ohio when Sonia was beginning her college studies and Esther was finishing high school.

Under Jim's tutelage, I had become more interested in the organ, and I decided the best way to improve my skills would be to go for a degree. I was accepted at the University of Akron as a candidate for a master of music in organ performance. I did indeed improve my skills, and I learned some very good organ literature and enjoyed most of my studies. I also discovered that, as a self-supporting adult with two part-time jobs, I was not able to devote myself as fully to my studies as I had as an undergraduate. However, I was happy with the progress I made, and I successfully completed my degree.

Meanwhile I had some interesting positions playing the organ in churches. At my first position back in Ohio, I worked with a choir director who did some things that did not seem very smart to me. For instance, he did not have the choir warm up their voices with vocal exercises. Then if a woman complained that she couldn't sing the high notes, he would tell her, "Okay. Then you're an alto."

I began taking notes about the things he didn't do well, and I thought about how I might do them better. At the same time, I had started accompanying and directing a group of about ten singers, who called themselves The Serenity Singers and sang at twelve-step meetings. Both of these activities helped give me confidence to apply for a position where I would play the organ and direct the choir at the same time.

Mogadore Christian Church was in need of an organist/director because the woman who had played the organ at that church for forty-two years had died a few days after playing for Christmas. She had been content with a small salary, considering herself partially a volunteer. I knew that most churches are unlikely to give generous raises, so the best time to get a decent salary is when beginning a job. In my interview, I told the committee that I wanted a salary about three times what they had been paying the previous organist/director. We eventually settled on a salary that was twice what they had given her. It was a friendly church, and I quickly became comfortable directing the choir from the organ bench. Besides the organ and the choir, I revived a handbell choir and also directed teenagers in performing a Christian play with music. I gave them my best, and I was happy in that position.

I had been there less than two years when I learned about an opening in a Methodist church in Akron that had a very fine Schantz organ and an exceptional music program. Even though I had to take a pay cut, I was happy to be part of a really fine music program.

However, the low pay was hard to live with, and within a couple of years, I found another organist/director position that paid much better.

There were several things I didn't like in my new position. The organ was an electronic instrument that imitated the sounds of a pipe organ, but it was quite unsatisfactory to my ears. I also had great difficulty selecting songs for the choir and the congregation, which was part of my job. As I read the words of the songs, I discovered that my sense of theology was quite incompatible with theirs, and I was actually feeling nauseous when I read the words of the songs. So about a year after I had started that job, I quit, thinking I was done with playing the organ in churches. By then, I had just enough piano students to support myself. I was happy to have Sunday mornings free, but I didn't really know what I wanted to do.

However, I was just getting to know Jay, and after a few months of conversations, I made the decision to move to Connecticut with him. At the time, I thought that if things didn't work out well, I would be able to return to Ohio. Things did not work out well, at least during the first few years, and I was not able to go back to Ohio. But eventually I found Connecticut to be a compatible long-term home.

══ CHAPTER 53 ══

Jay

Kent, Ohio, 1993–1994

I MET JAY ONE DAY IN 1993 when I ventured up to the second floor above my favorite natural food restaurant, the Red Radish. He had built a small shop out of plywood and two-by-fours, where he sold new age books and music CDs, incense, and Native American jewelry. I bought a pair of turquoise and silver earrings and started talking with Jay. He was a short, round, balding divorced man about my age (late forties) with long curly hair and a long beard—an original hippie from the '70s who was proud of the fact that he had never "sold out." That is to say, he had never had short hair or a conventional job.

A few days later when I was in his shop again, he showed me a blue paperback book titled Right Use of Will. "You may be interested in this book," he said. "The woman who channeled it had asked to receive a message from the highest source, so she was given this information, presumably from God. The whole book is about how God created humans with free will that was intended to lead them toward what they wanted and away from what they didn't want. However, there has been so much denial of true feelings that the will does not work as it was designed. The solution to this problem is for humans to get in touch with their feelings and express them as thoroughly as possible, especially all the feelings that we have denied, and then we can eventually come into the perfect balance that was God's intention in the first place."

I watched as his pudgy fingers expertly lit a cigarette. He inhaled and started blowing smoke rings. "That sounds like just the kind of book I've been looking for! I haven't wanted to believe that the tired old words of the Bible were God's last communication with humans. I'm excited to learn about this book that speaks to today's problems!" I told him.

Feeling and expressing my emotions was challenging. I was well acquainted with sadness and fear, but I could rarely feel anger, let alone express it, and I often had conflicting desires. For example, did I want a simple, nutritious, and inexpensive meal at home? Or did I want a generous plate of greasy food with Jay at his favorite eatery, Mike's Place, where the menu declared, "We serve breakfast all day because we never know what time you're going to roll your lazy ass out of bed"? I often ate there with him, even paying for his meal, just because I enjoyed his company.

Jay encouraged me to notice and express my feelings, although he tended to ignore or minimize any feelings or desires that didn't suit him. He also pointed out certain people who seemed real and authentic. As a way of trying to become more real and authentic, I started to imitate some of those people. In other words, I was trying to fake being real. Jay demonstrated his authenticity by using enormous amounts of profanity and by chasing every attractive young woman who appealed to him. Although he and I spent a lot of time together, we never became lovers.

Jay had previously been to Mystic, Connecticut, when his son was a student at Connecticut College nearby, and he had dreamed of living there. When we arrived in Mystic we saw a going out of business sign in front of a store quite similar to his. What a perfect opportunity!

Previous to our trip, Jay had repeatedly boasted to me, "In the right location, I could have a fucking awesome shop!"

When he told me of his attraction to Mystic, I suggested going to check it out. So there we were. Seeing the "going out of business" sign might have been a warning to me. If Peace of Mind, the new age bookstore in that location, was going out of business, what made me so sure that we would succeed with a similar business in the same location? I so much wanted to believe that we would do well that I tried to ignore my doubts.

I liked Mystic, and there was little to keep me in Ohio. I had been divorced for a long time, and my daughters had both moved away. I had recently resigned from my job as organist and choir director at a Lutheran church. I still had a good group of piano students and a few friends, but I wanted a new direction for my life.

After our trip to Mystic, Jay and I started making plans to open a shop there. We studied catalogs of books, jewelry, incense, new age music CDs, and tarot cards, selecting the very best to sell in our beautiful new store. We would be business partners. He had no money, but I had access to enough money to get started, mostly in the form of credit cards. He didn't see that as a problem. Once we opened our shop, we'd have plenty of money to live on and to pay back the credit cards! I wanted to believe that, but somewhere under the mountain of excitement, there was a deep pit of doubt and fear.

Why did I go along with him? Partly because I didn't want to let my fear stop me. I often repeated to myself the phrase, "Feel the fear and do it anyway." I hadn't learned how to distinguish between being fearful for good reasons and just being afraid to try something new. I also thought that I would learn from Jay how to predict what people wanted to buy (I had no clue) and how to run a "fucking awesome" business. Maybe I thought too that, in a new location with a new occupation, I could become a new person—magically transformed from the timid, conforming, obedient, churchgoing person I had been raised to be, into a bold, authentic, sexy, new age goddess.

I did go through a transformation, eventually, but it was not what I had fantasized.

CHAPTER 54

Rescued by the Church

Mystic, Connecticut, 1994

ARRIVING IN MYSTIC, I WAS surprised to see an unusual sign in front of the Catholic church less than two blocks from our shop. It was a rather permanent-looking sign, proclaiming in large letters, "Organist Needed." I had never before seen such a sign, and I was intrigued and curious. Why was that church so desperate for an organist? Was the priest hard to get along with? Was the organ in bad condition? Maybe they didn't pay very well?

Although I was not feeling friendly toward Christianity in general and I had resigned from an organist position just a few months before, I was feeling scared and desperate enough to consider working as a church organist again. After all, I had just invested all my available assets, as well as thousands of borrowed dollars, into stock for the store. I was committed to spending most of my time in the store with Jay. An organist job would be a way for me to earn some income while spending only a few hours a week away from the store. I realized that my anxiety about my financial situation was stronger than my antipathy toward the church. I would at least find out more about the organist that was needed at St. Patrick Church.

I made an appointment with Father Charles McGrail, who was friendly and welcoming toward me, although he was skeptical about my background as a divorced woman and suspicious about what kinds of books I would be selling in the nearby new age bookstore.

A modest Casavant pipe organ had been installed in the church a few years before. After one organist moved away after playing for only a year, they had somehow been unable to find a suitable replacement. As far as I could tell, the organ was adequate and in good condition; the priest seemed friendly and helpful; and best of all, the pay was about twice what I had received at my previous position, mostly in light of the fact that I would be expected to play for three Masses each weekend.

Father Charles agreed to try me out for the summer, and he introduced me to the choir director, a pleasant young woman named Theresa, who gave me all the information necessary for playing a Mass.

I was not familiar with the Catholic Mass, but I learned quickly, and I was soon comfortable with the pace and the ritual of the Mass. In my anti-Christianity mood I was happy that it was a Catholic church, as I "knew" that many of the beliefs of the Catholic Church were not true. I am quite sure that I would have had a harder time in a Protestant church, because my old conditioning would have tempted me to try to actually believe what the church was teaching. It was a little easier to resist believing the teachings of the Catholic Church.

Nonetheless, I wanted to shield myself as much as possible from taking in unwanted teachings of the church. For that purpose, I kept a paperback book beside the organ keyboard so that I could unobtrusively take in other information, instead of giving my attention to scripture readings and homilies. Whenever I had the sense that unwanted teachings or information were coming my way, my private internal alarm system would go off: Dogma alert! Dogma alert! And I would dive for cover into the book beside the organ. This served me well for several years.

In addition to being a much-needed source of income, being the organist in a large active church helped me to get quickly established as a member of the local community. As I write this, I am still the organist at St. Patrick Church, after twenty-five years, and still happy to be part of that community. I am convinced that the sign "Organist Needed" was put up for my benefit, and the church was waiting for me to show up.

CHAPTER 55

Inside Essence

Mystic, Connecticut, 1994–1995

OUR STORE, NAMED ESSENCE, WAS open seven days a week, from 10:00 a.m. to 6:00 p.m. In the morning, I would make coffee for Jay; he would light some incense and smoke a cigarette. I would walk to Citizens Bank and get some change for the cash register, and Jay would put out the sandwich board in hopes of attracting customers. Almost from the beginning, I enjoyed my time outside of the store more than time inside the store. Although I was in a constant state of fear, I experienced a sense of peace and sometimes even pleasure when I was out of the store, even if I was just walking to the bank or the post office.

We had a business account at Citizens Bank, and I also opened a personal account at the same bank. A few months later, horrified by the declining state of our business finances, I feared that my personal bank account would somehow get entangled in the bad fortunes of the store. I then opened an account in another bank, where I deposited fees I earned playing the organ for weddings and funerals, with the idea that Jay and Essence would not be able to touch that portion of my earnings.

The store was full of good things. We received frequent shipments of books on metaphysics and spirituality from our distributor, New Leaf. We had many wonderful books on meditation, affirmations, Native American spiritual practices, natural health, psychic phenomena, and the like. We had beautiful tarot cards, incense, Stannard wind chimes, and a large selection of jewelry.

All we needed was customers. People came into the store occasionally; there were a few customers who shopped periodically and some who ordered books that we didn't normally carry. I enjoyed greeting customers and helping them find what they were looking for.

However, on most days, there were very few people in the store. And once in a while, we had a day in which not a single customer entered the store.

We hosted psychic fairs every few months as a way of attracting customers. Jay found several women who did psychic readings, some with tarot cards and some with only their own intuition, and set up a fee-sharing deal with them on those days. We sent out mailings to let our customer base know about these events, and we put a big sign, with balloons, in front of the store to make it attractive and festive. We had moderate success with these, especially in good weather.

In the spring, after we had been in the store over six months, Anne, one of my favorite psychic readers, offered to give Jay and me a joint reading. She used a regular deck of playing cards. She dealt us each two cards. When I turned mine over, they were a 3 and a 5. Jay's cards were a Jack and a 10. She interpreted that as meaning that, for me, the store was a sign of poverty, and for Jay, it meant moderate prosperity. This certainly rang true for me.

Once when I'd heard Jay tell someone, "This is what I do for a living" (meaning his role as a shopkeeper), I had been taken aback. I hadn't said it out loud, but I'd said to myself, vehemently, He does not get his living from the store. He gets it from me! I had maxed out most of my credit cards and was able to pay very little on my debt. And it was getting worse rather than better.

One Saturday, there was an enthusiastic group of young men and women in their early twenties who exclaimed over things they found in the store and bought many items. When we closed the store for the evening, Jay put the cash in his pocket, as was his custom, and we went to the grocery store. He loaded up the cart with luxury items that we were not in the habit of buying, and I was dismayed. I had thought that our one day of excellent sales would help get the store's finances stabilized. I said to Jay, "We can't afford to spend so much here."

He said, "Your problem is that you don't spend enough. You need to spend more to attract a flow of abundance."

"I'm just not comfortable buying a lot of expensive things that we don't need."

He finally agreed to put some things back.

We continued to work on clearing our emotions. As much as I wanted to expose and release my feelings, I had been strongly conditioned to deny many of my feelings. In my family, expressing anger was never acceptable, so I learned to deny my anger as much as possible. I knew that I had a lot of resentment toward my mother, but a therapist I had gone to in my twenties had given me the idea that it was not appropriate to express that feeling, even in therapy. I also had a secret belief that I was so fundamentally flawed that even therapy would not help me. The main feeling that I was able to express was sadness, and I did a lot of crying. And no matter how sad I felt and how much I cried, I did not feel any release.

During the time I was with Jay, I was not yet ready to even become aware of my feelings of anger and self-protection, let alone do anything with them. I was aware of feelings of sadness, despair, helplessness, and hopelessness. And I internalized Jay's criticisms and blame when he said things like, "Your problem is that you're addicted to self-pity," and, "If it weren't for your negative attitude and lack of faith, we could have a thriving business."

I had been socialized to defer to men—to listen to them and to follow their dictates and suggestions and even their whims. I'd learned this model from my mother, from the mothers of my friends, and from other women around me. I didn't have any role models of strong, independent women that I could emulate. And since junior high school, I had been carefully trained as a piano accompanist. I knew how to follow a director. I had become sensitive to subtle cues from a soloist, and I took pride in my ability to follow. I had been taught that the job of an accompanist was to help make the soloist sound good and look good. The practice of following the person in charge had become a deeply entrenched habit with me. Even though I could see that Jay's business model was not working well, I had no ideas for how to improve it. And even if I had, I would not have known how to present them in ways that he could accept.

Occasionally, I would take an hour just for myself. My favorite getaway place was the main trail at Bluff Point State Park. I would stop by a small grocery store and pick up a soda and a packet of cookies and park my car. On the path near the water, in the fresh air and sunshine, I would feel a small part of myself coming alive, and I would look to my favorite tree to comfort the aching fear and sadness and loneliness I felt. Then I would go back to the store, reluctantly, but determined to give my best efforts to make a success of this risky venture.

Jay and I made an odd pair. We were both about the same height. He had short legs; powerful, muscular arms; a wide, round chest; and an even wider and rounder belly. His graying brown hair, thin on top, was long and curly; he kept it tied back with a rubber band. His beard was medium length and untidy, and he had deep semicircles under his eyes. I was long-legged, of slender build, with straight brown hair that I kept cut short and neat, and I had deep-set brown eyes, which were growing more and more frightened and sad. I dressed in modest and neat slacks and sweaters, always with earrings or some other jewelry. Jay's wardrobe consisted of two pairs of old jeans and a few T-shirts. He asked me to make him a pair of drawstring pants, which didn't do much for his image but gave him something to wear. I think he did not own any underwear.

When customers came into the store, they would see me, anxious and probably overeager to help them find something to buy. They would also see Jay, usually laidback, often with a cigarette in his mouth. Sometimes he would stub out his cigarette and go help a customer. He had an air of authority when he talked about books and other items in the store, and he could be very persuasive.

One day a female customer invited me to go for a walk with her. As we walked she said, "I've been going to twelve-step meetings of Adult Children of Alcoholics, and I've found them very beneficial. I think you might also like them."

"But my parents didn't drink," I said doubtfully.

She said, "That's okay. There are other people who go to those meetings whose parents didn't drink. Why don't you go try it out and see if it fits?" I think she had noticed how unhappy I looked.

I went to a meeting soon after that, and I was amazed that I had many of the same characteristics and problems as did people who had grown up with alcoholic parents. As soon as I heard "the problem," I knew that I belonged in this group. ("The problem" described characteristics of people who grew up in alcoholic or other dysfunctional families. These included feeling isolated and unsupported, being people pleasers, and feeling guilty when we stood up for ourselves.)

I attended meetings regularly, and I clung desperately to the sense of sanity and hope that I found in them. I was with other people who had wounds from their childhood that they were working to heal, and I felt supported and encouraged by their presence. I especially appreciated the opportunity to say what I needed to say without receiving comments from others. The rule of "no feedback" freed me from having to protect myself from other people's opinions and advice.

A few months after I started going to ACOA meetings and shortly after I had started therapy sessions, I was in the store with Jay one dreary afternoon. There were no customers in the store. Jay was lecturing me and blaming me, as usual. And I was allowing it, as usual. He said, "If you had more enthusiasm for the store, we would have a better business. You need to develop more self-confidence and not be the little mouse in the background. You're always such a 'nice' person, but 'nice' just doesn't do it. You need to be more real, more authentic."

As he continued his harangue, I didn't know how to answer him, so I said, "I'm going for a walk." I left the store for fifteen minutes.

At the time, I thought it was a weak and ineffective response to his lecturing and criticisms, but it was actually a turning point for me. I was beginning to trust myself and beginning to ignore the damaging blame and verbal abuse that Jay had been hurling at me.

In the spring, I was able to start working part-time with a landscaping crew while Jay stayed in the shop. Being outdoors in beautiful gardens and doing physical work brought peace and healing to me. At the same time, I was in therapy, and I continued to go to ACOA meetings, clinging to them like a lifeline.

Eventually, we closed the store. I was very relieved that I didn't have to deal with the store anymore, and I finally felt assured that I was not going to get deeper into debt. I also felt depressed and wondered how I was ever going to pay off the $20,000 credit card debt I had amassed.

CHAPTER 56

Blessings

O NE OF THE GREATEST BENEFITS of my life was what developed from being a partner in a failing business. At the time I was going through that difficult experience, I certainly did not think it was beneficial. I fervently wished for someone to rescue me, to pull me out of the ocean of depression and debt where I felt like I was drowning. Nobody came to rescue me, although some people encouraged me and helped me stay afloat while I laboriously made my way to the goals of mental health and financial solvency.

One reason I call this a beneficial event is that it provided me with the incentive to work on the deep psychological issues that had hampered me since early childhood. With the help of a good therapist and the support of other members of Adult Children of Alcoholics, I was able to examine many of the beliefs I had held since early childhood. I was also able to feel, explore, and eventually accept feelings of frustration, anger, and rage and to begin noticing my self-judgments, especially around sexuality and spirituality. Without the deep and uncomfortable depression brought on by having to deal with an unreasonable business partner in an unprofitable bookstore that was pulling me deeper and deeper into debt, I would not have been motivated to do the psychological work that eventually allowed me to live peacefully and comfortably with myself.

Another benefit from this situation was financial. Because I had run up a large debt and nobody was volunteering to rescue me, I had to find my own way out. By working through it, I became more skillful with finances. I learned to make a budget and stick to it. I discovered that, by finding opportunities and working hard, I was able to make progress with paying off my debts. And I learned how to make more money than

I would have believed possible, by charging more for my services and making sure that my work justified the price I was charging.

For example, after I was no longer needed on the landscaping crew, I was hired by a housecleaning service. After a few months of learning on the job, I started to find my own clients. Rather than charging by the hour, I charged them by the job. Thus, by working fast and efficiently, I could make more money in the time I had available. I also found more piano students. Each time I raised my rates, I also strove to improve my teaching so that people would feel like they were getting their money's worth.

Having financial stability eventually allowed me to participate wholeheartedly in the spiritual practice that I discovered.

Shortly after I had paid off my debts and had dealt with my most difficult issues in therapy, a rescuer actually appeared. I didn't know it at the time, of course, but my association with John Matthews would bring me significant benefits. Because of his help, I have gone from renting a one-bedroom apartment to owning a three-bedroom house.

As a result of these blessings, I have gained emotional health and mental clarity, as well as financial stability. I often think there was divine guidance helping me through my difficulties.

CHAPTER 57

An Unexpected Benefit

Mystic, Connecticut, 1998–2014

I FIRST MET JOHN MATTHEWS WHEN he asked me to meet him at the church to plan the music for his wife's funeral. A slender man with a full head of white hair and bushy white eyebrows, he announced, in a British accent, "I am the bereaved husband." I had a moment of confusion—I knew I had seen him at events of a club for single people that I belonged to. However, this was not the time to talk about that.

As we discussed the funeral, he had one unusual request. He wanted a trumpeter to play the "Grand March" from Aida, and he wanted to make sure that we would play the parts he liked best. He later explained that his wife's father had played the trumpet for operas in England.

A few weeks after the funeral, he phoned me to ask if I would like to go to a show with him. I declined. He asked again a few weeks later and persisted. Finally I told him that I had no interest in a romantic relationship, but maybe we could develop a friendship.

As we talked together, I learned that, although he and his late wife had been married for fifty years, they had lived separately for the last twenty—which explained why he had been going to singles groups even though he was technically still married.

As time went on, after telling me about his unhappy experiences in Probate Court dealing with his wife's estate, he said, "I have decided that the best way to keep my stepsons from getting their hands on my money is to own property jointly with someone outside the family, with right of survivorship. And I have decided that you are the person I want to own property with."

I was surprised. I also had several concerns. When I talked about the situation with my daughter Sonia, she pictured angry members of his family coming after me with knives. I wanted to be careful.

One Sunday, talking with him after church, I saw in his cloudy blue eyes a look that assured me that he really wanted the best for me.

After looking for a while, eventually we found a construction project that he liked. The builder had started work on a "raised ranch" house, and we arranged to buy it. John told me that we would have a one-sentence contract: We would each live our own life and not interfere with the other. He would live downstairs, and I would live upstairs. Although there was no real separation between our areas, he used the lower entrance, and I used the upper entrance, and we each maintained our privacy. We worked hard, painting the inside of the house ourselves and preparing the gardens for planting. He was a vigorous eighty-three, and I was fifty-eight.

I had a spacious three-bedroom house to use—a real luxury after my one-bedroom apartment. I had a nice bedroom, a room for massage therapy, and a separate meditation room. I was able to get a grand piano for my large living room, which helped me to attract a rewarding and profitable group of piano students.

I often invited John upstairs for lunch. We talked about various projects around the house and yard. And he told me some interesting stories about his life.

He was born in Liverpool, England. His mother died when he was only five years old, so he was sent to live with grandparents on the Isle of Man. He enjoyed freedom running around the countryside while his grandparents worked. After returning to Liverpool as a teenager, he joined the British Merchant Marines and was on ships during World War II. One ship he was on endured daily threats from a German warplane screaming through the sky above them at the exact time that the sun was in a position that made it difficult to see. Day after day, they were taunted by German planes. The captain of the ship, who was not a religious man, said to the men, "Hebrews 13:8." Puzzled, they found a Bible and read the verse: "Jesus Christ the same yesterday, today and forever."

Another story he was fond of telling happened when he was working for Electric Boat in Groton, Connecticut. Because of his technical expertise he had been asked to attend a meeting in Washington, DC. He was flown there in a small airplane and was told where to find the pilot for his return trip. Sitting in the small plane with the pilot, he looked at the fuel gauge and remarked that it was on empty. The pilot told him that was no problem and took off for the flight. After rising to the appropriate altitude and with instruments guiding them to their destination, the pilot fell asleep. Not knowing what to do, John looked out of the window and noticed that they were flying over Groton. He told the pilot, who, waking, said "Oh yes, it looks like Groton," and proceeded to land the plane. John was very glad to be on the ground.

He did well for a few years and then began to decline with Parkinson's disease and depression. He had several years of decreasing engagement with the world, and he died at home at age ninety-five, after twelve years in the house.

Why did John Matthews choose me to share some of his assets with? I think he was attracted to me; I think he liked my appearance and my cooperative personality and the fact that I was unattached. And I think being the church organist made me seem reliable, respectable, and maybe even a little bit holy. I would not have imagined that being a church organist would bring me this kind of benefit!

CHAPTER 58

Death of John Matthews

JOHN'S DAUGHTER JACKIE AND I had just finished a nourishing dinner, ending with gingerbread and lemon sauce when Jackie remarked about the beautiful sunset and then exclaimed, "I don't hear him breathing!" We were accustomed to hearing John's shallow breathing on the baby monitor, which we kept nearby. We went downstairs and found her father's body still warm but lifeless.

Two weeks earlier, John had been uncharacteristically willing to have a catheter inserted and to have a hospital bed brought in. The hospice nurse took me aside and said, "It will probably be only a week or two now. Someone will need to be with him all the time, so you must cancel your appointments."

I called Jackie, who had recently retired, and she agreed to come from her home in Wethersfield and stay as long as she was needed.

At first, John was still alert and continuing to eat custard and chocolate pudding and drink sips of apple juice and Carnation Instant Breakfast. Once he asked for a chocolate éclair and ate part of one. Freed from the need to get up to urinate, he was able to relax in bed, although a few times he insisted that he was going to get out of bed. "Lower the damn sides on my bed so I can get up!"

As he declined further, Jackie and I took turns sleeping on the couch in his room, to be there if he needed us and to give him liquid morphine every four hours. When we were both exhausted, I hired someone from a home health care agency to stay with him one night so Jackie and I could sleep. Even so, we were both up a time or two to check on him.

A hospice nurse came three or four days a week, and a home health aide from hospice came once every day to wash John, empty his urine bag, and make sure he was as comfortable as possible. Jackie didn't like to be left alone in the house with him, so I was able to find friends or hired help to keep her company when I needed to be out. Not only did I want to fulfill my obligations, but I also needed to take breaks from our deathwatch.

One evening, John was unusually talkative. He said, "Why are there so many people in my room?"

I asked him who was there, and he said, "These are guys I used to work with."

Thinking that maybe he was having visitors from beyond the grave, I asked, "Is Ed Cedar here?"

John replied, indignantly, "No! Ed Cedar is dead!"

When Jackie had been there over a week, we were still waiting for him to die. By then he was not eating and taking only occasional sips of water. A few days later, he became unresponsive. The day before he died, Jackie was feeling impatient and discouraged. "I've heard of people surviving months or even years in a coma," she said.

I reminded her that those people were being fed intravenously. I was sure that John couldn't last much longer without food.

On Tuesday afternoon, a lovely lady from the church choir came and sang to John and prayed with him. He didn't show signs of responding, but I believe that it comforted him in some way and may have helped to ease his passing a few hours later.

Although John never actually joined the Catholic Church, he had been given permission to have his funeral at St. Patrick Church and to be buried in St. Patrick Cemetery beside his wife. He was dressed in a new suit, and we made sure he had a handkerchief and a flashlight with him in the casket, as he had always wanted to have a flashlight and a handkerchief close at hand. And of course there was a trumpeter playing the "Grand March" from Aida at his funeral!

John had been adamant that he did not want to go to a nursing home; he wanted to die at home. I am very glad that I was able to help him get what he wanted. Attending to his needs was physically and emotionally exhausting, but I feel satisfied that we gave him good care. I am quite sure that my years of meditation and spiritual study helped me to meet the challenges of easing him through the final stage of life.

CHAPTER 59

My Career Finds Me

I DIDN'T KNOW IT THEN, BUT I was preparing for my career from early childhood. I thought that I was preparing to get married and live happily ever after. But at the same time, I was dutifully practicing the piano—scales, exercises, short pieces, longer pieces, and eventually whole sonatas by Beethoven. And when I reached my teens, my skills were advanced enough that I accepted the invitation to become our church's organist when Mrs. Genis moved away. When people asked me what I wanted to do when I grew up, I couldn't say. What I really wanted was to get married and live happily with a good husband supporting us, so planning a career was irrelevant.

There was a deeper reason I could not imagine a career for myself. I was very unsure about who I was, who I was supposed to be, and who I could be. Of course, I didn't realize this at the time because it was so pervasive in my thinking.

Using the Bible as a handbook for life was what my parents taught me every day. There were plenty of men in the Bible being prophets, fighting wars, building an ark, facing lions, writing letters, healing sick people, and on and on. What were the women doing? First there was Eve, who led Adam into disobeying God. And after that, the few women who were mentioned were notable only because of their relationship with a man, usually their husband.

Stories in the Bible about widows gave me the impression that losing one's husband to death was a terrible calamity for a woman and meant that she would be poverty-stricken and lonely for the rest of her life. Interestingly, I never read anything in the Bible concerning a man whose wife died, which led me to believe that husbands were much more important to wives than wives were to husbands. Similarly, there are numerous references to the sad plight of the fatherless, but I could find no reference to the motherless.

I experienced the imbalance of the sexes in my family. I watched my brother Will, four years older than me, running, jumping, climbing and generally enjoying himself. I have a vivid memory of him balancing on a plank supported several inches off the ground. When I took a turn to see if I could do it, Mom came along and told me, disapprovingly, "Girls don't do things like that." I saw my mother deferring to my father, asking him what she should do, having his coffee break ready for him, always ready to do whatever he said. He was also the chief disciplinarian; if we did something really bad, Mom would say, "Wait until your father hears about what you did." We knew that our offense was serious if we had to wait to receive the consequences from Dad.

Growing up in the shadow of the Good Book, as my father called the Bible, I had daily reinforcement of the idea that men were more valuable than women and that a woman found her place in the world only through a relationship with a man, and she had little power or even worth apart from that. I, therefore, believed, very deeply, that my true goal and role in life was to be the "helpmeet" for the man who would be my husband—that somehow I was not really a whole or valuable person until I had a husband to serve. By having a husband, my status in the world would rise exponentially, and I would be serving a purpose in the world.

Having a husband would also help to ease the feeling of shame I felt constantly about being female. Because God was male and all those who worked for God and found favor with God were male, I felt completely helpless in ever being able to find favor with God. The only woman in the Bible who seemed to have God's approval was Mary, the mother of Jesus, and she was best known for doing something no other woman could do—having a baby without having intercourse with a man. Her role seemed to be largely passive. She said, "Be it done to me according to your word." And when wondrous things happened in her life with her holy Child, she "pondered these things in her heart."

St. Paul counseled married woman to be subject to their husbands. In I Corinthians 14:34, "The women should keep silence in the churches.

For they are not permitted to speak, but should be subordinate, as even the law says. If there is anything they desire to know, let them ask their husbands at home. For it is shameful for a woman to speak in church."

And in Paul's first letter to Timothy:

> I desire then that in every place the men should pray, lifting holy hands without anger or quarreling; also that women should adorn themselves modestly and sensibly in seemly apparel, not with braided hair or gold or pearls or costly attire but by good deeds, as befits women who profess religion. Let a woman learn in silence with all submissiveness. I permit no woman to teach or to have authority over men; she is to keep silent. For Adam was formed first, then Eve; and Adam was not deceived, but the woman was deceived and became a transgressor. Yet woman will be saved through bearing children, if she continues in faith and love and holiness, with modesty. (I Timothy 2: 8–15)

I could not help but wonder why having female genitals made a person less capable, less intelligent, less trustworthy, or less persuasive than a person with male genitals.

In our church, the minister was always a man, and there was a group of men who conducted the serious business of the church. Women took care of children, taught Sunday school classes (but not the adult class), had monthly social meetings with cake and coffee, and held rummage sales to raise extra money for the church. They seemed to be following St. Paul's dictates, except for the injunction against braided hair and gold and pearls.

I tried valiantly to follow St. Paul's advice: "Do nothing from selfishness or conceit, but in humility count others better than yourselves. Let each of you look not only to his own interests, but also to the interests of others" (Philippians 2: 3–4). I could find plenty of people who were willing to let me consider them better than myself, but I never found anyone who wanted to consider me better than him or herself. It seemed like a very unbalanced teaching.

Years later, in therapy for depression, I realized that I was in the habit of doing something that I call "making myself dim." Very much like dimming the lights in a room, I kept tight control over my movements, my abilities, and my self-expression.

From early childhood on, I had been very restricted in my movements, as I was trying to avoid the scolding that would come from my mother if I let my panties show. Wearing short dresses that ended midthigh on my short legs did not allow much movement without exposing my underwear. Thus, I never participated in many youthful activities. And by the time I started school, my athletic abilities were woefully undeveloped.

I remember once visiting another girl in her home. When she started turning somersaults (something I didn't know how to do), her mother very matter-of-factly told her to put on some shorts. She did and continued turning somersaults. I felt both envious and enlightened—it seemed such an easy way to solve the problem of panties showing, which had been a major problem for me ever since I could remember.

In any case, I continued to be restricted in my movements, as I had not had the experience of most of my peers and, thus, was rarely welcomed into their games. I was often the first person out in dodgeball and the last person to be chosen on a kickball team.

I continually tried to turn down the volume on my emotions, another way of dimming myself. In my family, any child who expressed anger was reprimanded or punished. Until I was about six years old, I cried a lot, sometimes screaming with frustration and having the feeling that nobody understood me and, moreover, perceiving that my parents weren't even trying to understand me. After I started school, I was more likely to pout and mope sullenly. I risked punishment if I expressed my true feelings, so I came to believe that my feelings themselves were unacceptable, and I tried, unsuccessfully, to "get rid of them." The best I could do was turn down the volume on them or pretend they didn't exist, thus denying an important part of myself.

Even my intellect was subject to this dimming process. As long as my thoughts were acceptable to my parents and teachers, I could express myself. But if my thoughts and opinions were in conflict with the thoughts of adults in charge, I was careful to keep them reigned in. I also learned not to be too eager to answer a teacher's questions in class so as not to be labeled teacher's pet.

The most pervasive area of self-dimming was in my identification as female. I felt a constant, persistent feeling of shame in my genitals that had been passed on to me by my mother and other adults in my life. To be female meant being less than every male, in some unexplainable, permanent way. It meant having less authority, less value, less power and less freedom than a male in similar circumstances. I felt ashamed of my own femaleness and a lack of respect for feminine interests such as fashion and food.

Many years into adulthood, my therapist brightened my day once with a story about two young children. She had recently been with a friend whose children, a four-year-old boy and a three-year-old girl, were getting ready for a bath. As they undressed, the boy said, "I have a penis." The mother said to her daughter, "And you have a vagina." The little girl ran around pointing to her vagina and exclaiming, "I have a 'gina! I have a 'gina!" I was wishing that my femaleness had been affirmed in a similar way during my childhood.

But it wasn't just my physical being that I had a low opinion of. In many ways, I had a sense that I didn't have rights and didn't deserve things. When I first heard the phrase "excuse me for living," it made perfect sense to me. "Excuse me for living! Pardon me for taking up valuable space on this planet! I'll try to be whatever anyone wants me to be so I can justify my existence."

I had the impression that women were expected to be self-effacing, almost to the point of invisibility or nonexistence.

I did not know who I was. For a long time, I had a belief that I could develop whatever qualities I wanted (except maleness). And if I lacked some of the qualities I found attractive in other people, it was because I had not tried hard enough. In some way, I was usually on some kind of campaign to improve myself, trying to become at least a little bit more attractive or maybe more worthy.

In my teens, after hearing words from the Bible exhorting people to be humble and to consider others better than themselves and so on,

I had an idea that, if I carried those principles to an extreme, I would take the least desirable job so that the better jobs would be left for other people, and I would marry the least desirable husband so that the more desirable husbands would be available to other women. Of course, I did not see anyone around me living that way. And because I really didn't want to live that way, I discarded that idea. Still, it seemed to be the logical conclusion to many of the biblical injunctions.

At the same time that I was pondering words from the Bible and trying to make sense of them, I was also studying diligently in high school. I knew that I was capable of performing well in school, and my parents expected me to do what my teachers told me to do and to bring home good report cards. I observed that, in school, girls were at least as capable as boys. But I was so thoroughly indoctrinated with biblical patriarchy that I could scarcely imagine using my capabilities in any way other than being the supporting helpmate to my future husband.

Because I performed well in high school, and because part of my father's compensation for his work included generous college stipends for his children, my parents and I assumed that I would go to college after high school graduation. I wasn't sure what I would study at college. I knew I could succeed as a music major, so I applied and was accepted in the music department at the College of Wooster. Initially, I thought I would major in music education so that I would have a teaching certificate "to fall back on" if my husband were to die. Of course, I hadn't yet met a prospective husband, but I was still fervently hoping that I would. My piano professor suggested to me that majoring in piano performance, rather than music education, would be a good fit for me. So I followed his suggestion and majored in piano, with a minor in organ performance.

Included in my studies as a piano major was one course in piano pedagogy, and we were assigned beginning piano students from the community so we could practice teaching piano. I enjoyed working with individual students, teaching them to read music and encouraging them to play each composition well before moving on to learn a new one. I was comfortable in my role as a piano teacher; it felt natural, and it seemed to fit within the boundaries of a properly self-effacing woman.

Once I was out of college and engaged to be married, I needed a job. I applied at a bank and was about to take an entry-level teller position when I learned about an opening for a clerk at my favorite music store. I worked there for a year, teaching a few piano students on the side. That was a good job for me until my boss retired and closed the store. I then worked as a music therapist at a state hospital for people with intellectual disabilities. I led rhythm bands and choirs and attempted to involve lethargic patients in dancing or marching to recorded music.

When Terry was drafted into the army, I worked in a doughnut shop for a while and acquired a lifelong distaste for doughnuts. When he was stationed at Fort Leonard Wood, Missouri, I moved there, and we found a place to live together. Soon I was teaching piano lessons to children of army officers and playing the organ for chapel services on the base.

When Terry was sent to Vietnam, I continued to live there and continued the work I had begun, working all through my first pregnancy. I had discovered I was pregnant shortly after he went to Vietnam. I still had a dream of living happily ever after with my husband and our child. And I was using my skills as a piano teacher and organist to earn some money and pass the time while my husband was away.

A few years later, when we moved to Kent, Ohio, where Terry was a professor at Kent State University, I bought two pianos for my basement piano studio and got started teaching again. Teaching at home worked well for me when I had young children, although I still had to get a babysitter when Esther was very young. I enjoyed my teaching, but I also had dreams of having a "real" career. As the spouse of a professor, I had the opportunity to take any courses I chose, tuition free. I decided it was time to pursue my interest in psychology.

After becoming disenchanted with the psychology department, I enrolled in a master's program in counseling, which was in the school of education. By the time I completed the course, the department was going through reorganization, and my marriage was falling apart. Thus, I did not feel well prepared to jump into a new career. After a few attempts, I decided that I could integrate some of the skills I had learned in counseling into my piano teaching. I did that, and I was happy with the results. About the same time, I started to take a deeper interest in the organ.

A few years later, I decided that the best way to improve my skills as an organist was to study for a degree. I enrolled at the University of Akron and completed a master's degree in organ performance.

In my early fifties, I was a piano teacher and a church organist, but I wanted to do something I could feel genuinely passionate about. I decided that becoming a hospice volunteer was something I could do with passion. I appreciate the hospice philosophy of giving people choices at the end of life, and I was hoping to help people's final months to be more comfortable than my father's last days had been. I also hoped that I would be privileged to catch glimpses of the next world as I sat with those who were preparing to enter it. That hasn't happened, but I have found satisfaction in my work with hospice.

Shortly after getting involved with hospice, I started training to become a massage therapist. I planned to do massage in the mornings and teach piano lessons in the afternoons after school. I was happy doing that for about twenty years and have now retired from massage therapy.

I have finally discovered in the last fifteen years that my career as a piano teacher and a church organist is genuinely satisfying. No longer do I believe that am I just taking the easy route and using the skills I learned early in life only because I don't have anything better to do. I love working with individual students, relating to them, helping them achieve their musical goals and introducing them to wonderful music. I am also very happy being a church organist, helping to create a reverent atmosphere in church, encouraging enthusiastic singing, and being with many devoted people. I believe that I am helping to make the world a better place.

CHAPTER 60

What I Like about Church

Me as a very young church musician

THERE ARE MANY THINGS THAT I enjoy and appreciate about being the organist at St. Patrick Roman Catholic Church in Mystic. I like playing the sweet-voiced Casavant pipe organ. I like playing soft music as parishioners arrive to spend time in prayer and contemplation, some of them arriving more than thirty minutes before the service begins. I thrill to the sound of many voices singing enthusiastically along with the organ. I love accompanying the choir, a talented and friendly group of about twenty singers, led by an excellent choral director. And I have had the privilege of working with several excellent, devoted priests.

I like to think that the organist position at St. Patrick Church was made to order for me. Not only are all the duties uniquely suited to my skills, but it also seems as though the church was waiting for me to show up when I did. The lovely pipe organ had been purchased from another church in Connecticut a few years before, but when I arrived, the church did not have an organist. They had posted a large sign in front of the building, "Organist Needed." I was astonished—I had never seen a sign like that. After interviewing for the position, I was hired provisionally for the summer. I have now been there more than twenty-five years.

I love being in an atmosphere of reverence. I try to enhance the quiet prayerful mood as people come into church and pray silently. Another one of my favorite times is right after everyone has received Communion and there is often a holy hush throughout the church.

I like being around people who are well dressed, quiet, and respectful. I like that people sit still and don't make unnecessary noise or commotion in church and that they teach their children to do the same.

I enjoy being with large groups of people in church each weekend. I see children growing up and couples growing old together or coming to church alone after the death of a spouse. I am entertained by a toddler gleefully escaping from his parents. I am touched by the sweet devotion of a husband and wife who are both mentally handicapped. I make up stories about people I see frequently but never speak to.

I like getting paid for going to church. When I first started working at St. Patrick Church, I depended on my modest salary for the most basic essentials. I still appreciate being paid for doing something that I enjoy and can do with very little effort, thanks to years of lessons and two degrees in music.

I have discovered that I can appreciate the many opportunities to hear scriptures, homilies, creeds, and prayers and to observe my own responses to them. Hearing them week after week is helping me to clarify my thoughts about Christian teachings and what my objections are to some of them. I am able to contemplate the beliefs of the Christian church from the perspective of one who does not share many of the basic beliefs. This has proved to be an invaluable source of inspiration for me as I write this memoir.

CHAPTER 61

Getting Mom off My Back

I HAD BEEN IN THERAPY FOR severe depression for a year when I went to visit my mother in Illinois. As soon as I was in her house, my brain got fuzzy, and I turned into her robot daughter. That was the only way I knew how to relate to Mom, even though I was in my fifties!

I had never told her that, when I was twenty-five, I had decided I no longer wanted to call myself a Christian. I was sure she would not be able to accept or even understand why I would do such a thing. She and Dad had given their children a good Christian upbringing, and Mom was absolutely certain that Christianity was the only way to salvation. So it would make no sense to her for any of her children to choose anything other than Christianity.

At Mom's house, everything has to be done her way. Dishes must be washed in the dishpan. Strawberries must be sliced vertically, not horizontally. The table must be set properly. Once before dinner, after I had arranged everyday stainless utensils on the white tablecloth beside the bone china plates, she quietly removed the everyday silverware and replaced it with the silver-plate silverware. And of course on Sunday, anyone in her house must go to church with her.

On that visit, going to church was particularly excruciating. I felt like Mom's show-and-tell exhibit as she proudly took me around for her friends to see what a good Christian mother she was. I had to sit beside her while she piously recited the prayers. She nodded in agreement when the minister denounced homosexuality. I felt completely alienated.

When I told my therapist how painful it had been, she asked why I went to church with Mom. Why didn't I just tell her that I preferred to stay home? I answered that I still needed to be part of my family. Going to church was such a central part of our family tradition that I thought, if I refused, I would be excommunicated from the family.

After several years of intensive work in therapy, much of it focused on Mom and my relationship with her, one day I came in for a session filled with rage at Mom. Talking, shouting, cursing—nothing seemed to make the least difference. I was disheartened. I wanted to get over my anger and rage.

My therapist then asked, "Can you think of a purpose your rage might be serving?"

Oh! Yes, I could! My rage was keeping me from letting Mom tell me how to live my life! Once I recognized the purpose of my rage, I felt miraculously free and powerful and even comfortable with it. I realized that it was not the rage that was bothering me; it was my judgment that I should not have rage. When I understood what it was for, I felt thankful to it for taking care of me.

CHAPTER 62

Beginning Sahaj Marg Spiritual Practice

Mystic, Connecticut, 1999

SOON AFTER GRADUATING FROM COLLEGE and getting married, I decided that I no longer wanted to consider myself a Christian. My husband had no objection. I was hoping to find something to replace Christianity in my life, so I started looking for some form of spirituality that would appeal to me. After a few years, I discovered Yogananda's Autobiography of a Yogi. I read it with avid interest and wished that I could have known Yogananda in person. However, I felt reassured by the fact that a person of such great spiritual stature had been alive during my lifetime. Learning about spiritual truth from a modern-day person appealed to me ever so much more than trying to understand the ancient, confusing, and possibly outmoded teachings of the Bible. I carefully studied Yogananda's teachings for a while and tried to meditate, but I found it so difficult to still my mind that I came to the conclusion that I was just not the kind of person who was capable of meditating.

After twenty-five more years of reading books, talking with people, and attending seminars and gatherings, I still had not found a satisfactory spiritual practice. I went through a turbulent period of life, during which I examined old feelings and beliefs with the help of a therapist and worked hard to get out of debt. When I was feeling more stable, I again had a desire to learn to meditate. One day, I saw a small notice in the newspaper. "There will be an introduction to meditation at the Old Lyme Library on Sunday afternoon at 3:00. All are welcome."

There were half a dozen people in the room when I arrived. They greeted me warmly. I looked at books and pictures set up on a table. A vibrant white-haired woman noticed that I was looking at a photo of a distinguished and kind-looking Indian man. She said, "Hi! My name is Marsha. I see that you are looking at a picture of our spiritual guide. His name is Parthasarathi Rajagopalachari. We call him Charlie."

I thought Charlie was an unusually casual name for such a revered spiritual leader. A few minutes later, I discovered that I had misunderstood; he was called Chari, from the last part of his name, Rajagopalachari.

More people came in, and soon we were all sitting on chairs in a circle. Marsha started her talk by saying, "We are here to talk about the practice of Sahaj Marg, which means 'the natural path.' It was started in India and has spread to many parts of the world. We who have been practicing have found it to be extremely beneficial."

I noticed several people in the room nodding emphatically.

"The practice is very simple. We sit silently and meditate on divine light in the heart. We don't try to see the light; we just suppose that it is there, and we think continuously of divine light in the heart. The recommended time for meditation is one hour; many people start with a shorter period and work up to a full hour. In addition, we have group meditation on Sunday mornings and Wednesday evenings. Now Jim will talk about cleaning, which is another aspect of the practice."

The process of cleaning, as Jim described it, is very simple. "In the evening, after the day's work is done, sit for half an hour with eyes closed and imagine that all complexities and impurities are going out behind you, like smoke or vapor."

After Jim finished talking, I raised my hand and commented, "I am so happy to learn about cleaning. I've noticed that I keep building up more and more emotional baggage, and I never knew what to do with it!"

One unique feature of Sahaj Marg is the transmission given by the master. He has the ability, passed down from one master to the next, to send divine energy to receptive hearts in a form they can use. The master often does this when sitting in meditation with large groups of people, and those present often feel overwhelming peace and love. One does not need to be physically present with the master, as distance is not a barrier. In addition, there are individuals in many parts of the world who have been trained and given permission to act as conduits for transmission. They are called prefects.

At the time, Marsha was the only local prefect, and over the next few days she assisted me in getting started with my practice of Sahaj Marg.

Amazingly, there was no charge for anything. At gatherings, there was a suggested donation amount, but it was not required. Preceptors and other volunteers did their work without compensation and considered it a privilege as well as a duty.

Once I settled into the practice, I meditated every morning, sometimes as long as an hour. I was taught to begin my meditation period with the Sahaj Marg prayer: "O Master, thou art the real goal of human life. We are yet but slaves of wishes, putting bar to our advancement. Thou art the only god and power to bring us up to that stage." I didn't understand it then, and I still don't understand it now, but I was happy to say it, silently, and puzzle over its meaning.

In the evening, I practiced cleaning, during which I imagined all of the day's complexities going out of me and disappearing behind me like smoke or vapor. I liked ending the day by cleaning and letting go of everything that had occupied my mind and my time that day and preparing for a restful night of sleep without the intrusion of unfinished business.

I was very happy to practice this form of meditation for more than fifteen years. It served me well, until I came to a point in my life when I felt the need of something different.

CHAPTER 63

India

I HAD A GREAT DESIRE TO go to India to spend time in the presence of my spiritual teacher, known as Chari. After I had been in the practice for eight years, I was determined to go to India for the celebration of Chari's eightieth birthday in July 2007. For a long time, I had been putting aside twenty dollars a week for that purpose. Finally, it was happening! I had my passport, visa, and travel plans, which I had made with three traveling companions. I had put together a wardrobe of modest clothing suitable for a hot climate—long pants, long skirts, long-sleeve shirts, and a wide-brimmed hat to shield my pale skin from the tropical sun. I had a pillowcase ready to stuff with clothing to use as a pillow for what I knew would be very simple sleeping arrangements.

On the third and final flight of our long trip, we landed at the airport in Coimbatore and took one of many specially chartered buses to the celebration grounds of Tirrupur.

Because a huge crowd of devotees was expected for that event, Chari had given permission to have the celebration at Tirrupur. Crews of volunteers had worked for months to transform a large, hilly plot of arid land into a place to hold a weeklong celebration for fifty thousand people. They had worked for months putting together electricity and water infrastructure and gathering equipment needed for housing, feeding, and sheltering all who planned to attend the gathering. And they had succeeded amazingly well.

I stayed in a "comfort dorm," where fifty cots were set up in each room under a huge tent with electric fans mounted in the ceiling. Toilets and showers were a short hike away from the sleeping area. Meals were served at the thatch-roofed dining pavilion, where rice and well-seasoned beans and vegetables were served out of huge vats. Somehow, meals were always ready on time, and we never had to stand in line for more than ten or fifteen minutes before taking a metal plate to be filled by the sari-clad kitchen ladies. I felt satisfied and well fed after each meal. I was grateful that, in consideration for people accustomed to bland food, they used only small amounts of the hot spices that are customary in South Indian food.

At the center was a huge tent, big enough to shelter about forty thousand people if they all squeezed close together. I went at least an hour before each scheduled meditation so that I would have a place to sit cross-legged on the floor. I took a couple of small towels with me to cushion my bony feet on the hard ground and also to wipe the sweat off my face. It was very hot.

Meditation was scheduled for two or three times each day. I would arrive an hour or two before the meditation was scheduled to begin, and already the huge meditation tent was beginning to fill up. We sat quietly waiting. Although I found it hard to get comfortable, I was very happy to be there. Sometimes during meditation, I was distracted by my uncomfortable body or by my thoughts, but I still had the sense that I received great benefit just from being there.

After one exceptional meditation, I wrote in my diary, "Meditation felt like waves and layers of bliss, rolling over us and filling all to capacity." Another time I was so moved that tears were running down my cheeks. And I often felt full of love and spiritual blessings.

In addition to periods of meditation, we had talks and performances of music and dance. Master gave several talks in spite of the fact that he was suffering from a cold and had throat problems. During one memorable exchange after one of his talks, one follower said to him, "I'm ashamed to be an American," a feeling which I also sometimes share.

Master responded, "You must not be ashamed but, rather, work to be the best you can be and improve what you can."

I was deeply moved by a performance of part of the Mozart Requiem, presented by an international orchestra and chorus of nearly two hundred people—French, German, British, American, Russian, Chinese, and Iranian, as well as people from many parts of India. There was also a fine Russian ensemble whose original songs moved me to tears.

Disappearing into the superfine energy of fifty thousand dedicated spiritual seekers meditating together in the presence of our beloved master, Parthasarathi Rajagopalachari—that was what I had come for, and it greatly exceeded my expectations.

In other years I went several times to the ashram in Manapakkam, a suburb of Chennai, India. I thoroughly enjoyed walking around the grounds of the ashram, which were being lovingly maintained by devoted volunteers. A large open-air meditation hall had been built some years before, and there was plenty of space for sleeping on the floor under the meditation hall. Here is a description of one of my experiences there:

> I am walking on one of the wide paths around the beautiful meditation hall of the Sri Ram Chandra Mission in Manapakkam. There are trees, potted flowering plants, areas of grass, and a few life-size statues of Hindu gods. The sun is blasting me, even though I am wearing a wide-brimmed hat and long sleeves and long pants. As I stop for a swig out of my water bottle, I marvel at my good fortune to be here. The grounds and especially the meditation hall feel highly charged with beneficial spiritual energy. I want to soak up as much as I possibly can.
>
> An hour before group meditation is scheduled to begin, I leave my sandals on one of the many shoe racks outside the meditation hall and join the line of people climbing the wide marble stairs. They are hot now, under the sun; I will experience them as cool and slippery when they are being washed during the night by hardworking volunteers. When I was getting ready to come to India, I asked my prefect, Marsha, if I should volunteer to work in the kitchen or some other job. She replied that I would probably need to focus on taking care of myself. She was right.
>
> When I arrive in the meditation hall, I find a place to sit on the women's side and begin quietly meditating.

From time to time, I open my eyes and observe what is going on around me. Although the open-air meditation hall is large enough to hold about five thousand people, with many of them sitting cross-legged on the floor, more people keep coming in. I see guards assisting people in crowding together as much as possible, while keeping the aisles clear. Everyone wants to be here and to be ready when Master arrives.

Chari arrives in a golf cart, accompanied by his grandson and granddaughter and a few other people. He is wearing a loose cotton shirt and pants. The first thing he does is hang a garland of flowers on the portrait of Lalaji (the first master of the Sahaj Marg practice) and one on the portrait of Babuji (the second master). Once he has completed that, he sits on the special chair on the platform at the front of the meditation hall and looks around at the people assembled. There is something so profound in his glance that I feel a sense of peace, and also I feel tears forming in my eyes. Soon he says, "Please begin meditation."

I have (mostly) profound meditation for about an hour.

At the end, Chari says, "That's all."

We have been encouraged to spend time after meditation contemplating what we have experienced. I often find that helpful. Sometimes I don't recognize what I experienced during meditation until afterward, so I am happy for this time of reflection.

Chari again looks slowly around the large assembly. I get the impression that he is connecting with each person there. He then gives a short inspirational talk.

Leaving the meditation hall, I pass by the statues of lions on each side of the stairway, reminding us to be vigilant and intense in our spiritual practice. I am happy to be here, and I want my practice to be the very best it can be.

CHAPTER 64

Leaving Sahaj Marg

Connecticut, 2017

A FEW YEARS AFTER I WROTE the previous glowing description of my experiences with Sahaj Marg, I began to feel dissatisfied with Sahaj Marg. I was sad when the living master, Parthasarathi Rajagopalachari, died in 2014, but I was ready to accept his successor, Kamlesh Patel. I had heard Kamlesh speak a few times, and I was impressed by his sincerity and dedication. Soon after he became the master, (he preferred to be called daaji, which means "uncle," specifically the younger brother of one's father), he started a movement called "Heartfulness" in which we were encouraged to find ways to talk to as many people as possible about Sahaj Marg. Public information meetings were arranged. I was very uncomfortable. It felt like I was being asked to be a missionary.

I continued in the practice, but it was becoming increasingly uncomfortable for me. During my daily meditations, I spent a lot of time just sitting with my runaway thoughts. I seldom had the deep satisfaction of losing myself, as I remembered from earlier times. As I looked for help, the main suggestion I found was Babuji's comment, "Treat thoughts as uninvited guests." Many hours I sat thinking about what I would do if I found uninvited guests wandering around in my house. I couldn't just ignore them! Was that something that other people would do? How was this piece of advice supposed to help people go deep into meditation? I pondered that over and over as I sat uneasily with my thoughts running rampant.

During group meditation, I tried to let go and melt into the peaceful atmosphere of the group. Sometimes I succeeded. But very often I felt like I needed to defend myself against the transmission that was coming through the prefect who was leading the meditation. I also increasingly felt that there was no place for my emotions in Sahaj Marg. The emotional side of me felt like it was being told, "Just shut up and meditate." I was unable to find a satisfactory answer that would allow me to continue my practice comfortably.

I wanted to break away from Sahaj Marg, but I was afraid of losing the social connections that I valued. I also wondered if I was doing the right thing for me. I found a therapist who understood my predicament, and I had weekly sessions with her for several months. She listened carefully to me, and she encouraged me to dig into the painful places that I tended to avoid. She also encouraged me to proceed with meditation in my own way.

After months of therapy, I was convinced that breaking with Sahaj Marg was the right thing, the healthy thing for me to do. I told people that I was taking a break from it, and I have not been tempted to go back. Even though I know I would be welcome at group meditation, I have not had a desire to go there.

CHAPTER 65

Thoughts about the Bible

A T THIS POINT IN MY story, I want to examine some of the thoughts and questions I have had about the Bible. Some of my questions have been with me since early childhood, and others have grown out of my thinking and experiences as an adult.

I'll begin with the famous prayer attributed to Jesus.

Reflecting on the Lord's Prayer

By the time I was seven years old, I could recite the Lord's Prayer by memory. After all, we said it in church every Sunday. I stumbled over one hard word (temptation), usually saying "lead us not into 'tation." But otherwise, I knew the whole prayer. Did I understand what I was saying? Probably not very much.

Over the many years since then, I have had ample opportunity to consider this prayer and what it means to me. I know this prayer is well known to most Christians, and many derive strength and comfort from reciting it. However, I have a number of questions and misgivings about the prayer:

- Our Father
  I resist thinking of the deity as a masculine parent. I much prefer the Christian Science interpretation, as put forth by Mary Baker Eddy, "Our Father-Mother God, all harmonious." I love that phrase and sometimes repeat it to myself, almost as a mantra.
- Who art in Heaven

- This phrase encourages me to think of the divine as far away from me. I prefer to think of God as present everywhere, particularly with me.
- Hallowed be thy name
  If the divine presence is everywhere and in everything, it is likely that many names can be associated with Him.
- Thy Kingdom come, thy will be done, on earth as it is in Heaven
  Is this a petition to the Almighty, or is it a reminder to earthlings that it is our responsibility to live according to the highest principles we know?
- Give us this day our daily bread
  I would hope that we have such an intimate relationship with our heavenly parent that we don't have to beg Him for our most basic necessities. Certainly, as children, we expected our earthly parents to provide us with our daily needs, without our having to ask or beg. Should we expect any less from our heavenly parent?
- And forgive us our trespasses as we forgive those who trespass against us
  Most of us are on shaky ground here. If our divine parent is limited to forgiving us to the extent that we forgive others, that may indeed be a strict limitation. I certainly hope, and believe, that the divine spirit is infinitely more compassionate and forgiving than our often-misguided human nature.
- Lead us not into temptation
  Why do we have to beg God not to lead us into temptation? What kind of God would deliberately lead us into temptation? We are fully capable of tempting ourselves with our own desires for things and experiences that may not be in our best interests. Do we really believe that God will lead us into temptation unless we beg Him not to? In 2017, Pope Francis suggested that the wording of this phrase should be changed to, "Let

me not fall into temptation." I had another thought once when contemplating a table of rich desserts at a buffet: "Lead me away from temptation!"

- But deliver us from evil
  Again, it seems strange to beg God to deliver us from evil. Shouldn't that be God's natural inclination?
- For Thine is the Kingdom and the Power and the Glory forever
  By this we are acknowledging that God is in charge and powerful and eternally glorious.

CHAPTER 66

Jesus

I AM SUSPICIOUS ABOUT, AND TEND to doubt the truth of many of the stories of "Magic Jesus" in the Bible. These include:

- virgin birth
- angels and shepherds and wise men
- turning water to wine
- casting out demons
- walking on water
- feeding five thousand people with five loaves and two fishes
- ascending visibly into heaven
- sitting on the right hand of God (if God is everywhere, where is His right hand located?)

However, the essence of Jesus, as I understand it, fills me with love and inspiration and yearning. The love and compassion of Jesus is evident in many of the stories and sayings attributed to him:

- Healing people who were sick or blind or handicapped
- Eating with a tax collector—Jesus showed love and compassion to everyone he met. He did not share the general prejudice against tax collectors and was willing and happy to eat with a tax collector when he was invited.
- Welcoming a gift from a "loose woman"—Rather than judging her for her past behavior, Jesus welcomed the loving spirit of her gift.
- Inviting fishermen to join him—I believe that Jesus perceived the willingness of the rough, ordinary fishermen that he chose as disciples.

- Welcoming children—When others tried to send the children away, Jesus invited them and shared his love with them.
- Respecting the law but not being bound by it—When Jesus was moved to help someone with love, he did not consider that he was going against the strict religious laws of his day. Some people criticized him for healing on the Sabbath for instance, but that didn't stop him.
- Overcoming prejudice—When a Canaanite woman begged Jesus to heal her daughter, he told her that he had been sent only to the lost sheep of the house of Israel. When she again asked for help, he replied, "It is not fair to take the children's bread and throw it to the dogs." She answered, with wisdom and/or desperation, "Even the dogs eat the crumbs that fall from the master's table." Jesus praised her for her faith and healed her daughter.
- Calming fears—On several occasions, Jesus calmed the fears of his disciples. Among these were when they were in a boat on a stormy sea, when his friend Lazarus died, and when they were surrounded by hostile men in the garden of Gethsemane.
- Praying—Jesus often went off by himself to pray, thus setting an example for us.

CHAPTER 67

What Is in the Bible?

MANY PEOPLE ARE FAMILIAR WITH a few parts of the Bible—Adam and Eve in the garden of Eden; Noah and the flood; some of the Psalms, especially Psalm 23, "The Lord is my shepherd"; the stories about the birth of Jesus (although the two accounts do not agree with each other); some of the parables of Jesus; the story of Jesus's crucifixion and resurrection; and some of the letters of St. Paul.

There are other parts of the Bible that most people are not aware of. The verses that give instructions for selling one's daughter into slavery (Exodus 21:7) and recommend stoning to death one's stubborn and rebellious son (Deuteronomy 21:19) are largely ignored, thank goodness! There are also the strange stories of Balaam's talking ass (Numbers 22:28); Jacob being tricked into marrying Leah (Genesis 29:22); Abraham telling Abimelech that his wife, Sarah, was his sister; and many other stories that are of little use for guidance or comfort. But because they are in the Bible, people pay attention to them, at least those who read the Bible carefully.

Besides the Ten Commandments, there are numerous (more than six hundred!) laws given to the Israelites concerning sacrifices in the temple, dietary restrictions, cleansing of a woman after menstruation or childbirth (Leviticus 12:2), what kind of clothing is permissible (Leviticus 19:19), and even outlawing tattoos (Leviticus 19:28)! Apparently the God of the Bible wanted to regulate people's daily life as much as possible. Most people today pay no attention to the majority of those laws.

However, there are other parts of the Bible that are useful for inspiration and guidance. Many people find comfort in their favorite Psalms. Many also look to the parables and sayings of Jesus for help in their daily lives. These are the parts of the Bible that are most often read aloud in churches.

It is comforting to believe that God cares about us (Matthew 10:31), useful to be reminded not to worry about our daily existence (Matthew 6:34), good to be reminded to be kind to each other, and helpful to follow Jesus's example of frequent prayer. I find inspiration in stories in which Jesus shows kindness to people who were commonly ostracized in his society.

Some parts of the Bible I consider very good, but other parts are of little use. Still other parts are negative and, to my way of thinking, should not be included in a book of inspiration. But how does the average reader or even the more discerning reader distinguish between the useful and the harmful? How can one sort out what might actually be true and which stories are exaggerations or completely fictional? Even the greatest theologians do not agree, and regular people are often divided, sometimes violently, about what the Bible means and what it is telling them to do.

If this is really the Word of God, I could hope that it would be less ambiguous and much clearer and easier to apply to peoples' everyday lives.

CHAPTER 68

Good and Evil in the Bible

VERY EARLY IN THE BIBLE, the concepts of righteousness and evil become important ideas. Often the way these words are used leads us to the conclusion that some people are totally righteous, or at least mostly righteous, while others are so unrighteous that the only thing God knows to do with them is to destroy them. The first example of wholesale condemnation begins in Genesis just before the Great Flood, when God "saw that the wickedness of man was great in the earth, and that every imagination of his thoughts was only evil continually" (Genesis 6:5). Is it really possible that all the people of the earth were so thoroughly entrenched in evil that they had no redeeming good qualities and no hope of improving?

It seems to me that God (or more accurately, the writer who attributed these thoughts to "God") is setting a very bad example of black-and-white thinking—all or nothing. In today's world, there are people who commit crimes, who do destructive acts, and who are sometimes hateful and aggressive toward other people. Yet many of the same people can be helpful to their friends and family and can be kind to animals and children. And some of these people lead the lives of upstanding citizens with only one glaring exception. We can consider some acts to be wicked, but that does not mean that the perpetrator of the acts is completely evil.

However, according to the Bible, God justified sending a flood to destroy nearly all the people of the earth on the basis of their wickedness.

On the other hand, "Noah was a righteous man and perfect in his generations, and Noah walked with God" (Genesis 6:9). Here is more black-and-white thinking. How could it be possible that everyone else in the world was totally evil and Noah and his family were totally good?

Similarly, when Abraham's nephew Lot pitched his tent near Sodom, we are told "The men of Sodom were wicked, great sinners before the Lord" (Genesis 13:13). When God told Abraham that He (God) was going to destroy Sodom and Gomorrah because of their wickedness, Abraham bargained with God, asking, "Wilt thou indeed destroy the righteous with the wicked?" (Genesis 18:23).

Eventually God agreed not to destroy Sodom if ten righteous persons could be found there. However, we are not given any criteria by which God (or Abraham) determined who was wicked and who was righteous. Again, we are led to believe that some people are all wicked, with no redeeming qualities and no possibility of change. Others are righteous. Period.

I believe that this kind of thinking has caused untold suffering in the world. We would presume that God, creator of the world, has infinitely greater power and imagination than any human possesses. And if the only thing God knows to do with huge groups of wicked people is to destroy them, is it any wonder that humans have often inflicted destruction on whole groups of people considered to be unrighteous or somehow undesirable? If destroying the wicked is the best that God knows how to do, humans are only following the example of their creator and guide. In fact, by following God's example, people often believe that they are doing the right thing.

However, it's not reasonable or even logical that Almighty God, infinitely powerful, the creator of all the marvels of the world, would have such a poverty of resources and imagination that His only solution to evil in the world is wholesale destruction of the evildoers. Let us not follow the example of the Bible!

CHAPTER 69

More about Righteousness

THE BIBLE BOOKS OF I and II Kings and I and II Chronicles tell about the kings of Israel and of Judah. Many of the kings reportedly "did what was evil in the sight of the Lord." One of the first to gain that notoriety was Jeroboam, the son of Nebat (1 Kings 11–13). Apparently, his primary sin was that of building two golden calves for the people to worship. Some later kings followed the same practice and were reported as "doing evil in the sight of the Lord."

Kings who "did right in the eyes of the Lord" engaged in much killing. For example, in 2 Kings 14, Amaziah, king of Judah, who was lauded for doing right in the eyes of the Lord, killed the servants who had killed his father but allowed their children to live. He also killed ten thousand Edomites in the Valley of Salt. (And he was not using a machine gun—it was all with swords and daggers and maybe bow and arrow!) However, his righteousness did not save him from being defeated by Jehoash, king of Israel (2 Kings 14:1–20). Similarly, his son, Azariah, did what was right in the sight of the Lord when he was king of Judah; nevertheless, for some reason that is not explained, the Lord smote him with leprosy (2 Kings 15:1–5).

In the Old Testament, the main component of "righteousness" seems to consist of the proper worship of God—offering the prescribed sacrifices of burnt animals on the proper altars dedicated to Jehovah, the jealous god of that group of people.

Fortunately, among the more than six hundred laws given to the Israelites, there are a few laws concerning humane treatment of the poor and needy, the widow, and the fatherless, giving some helpful rules of conduct, instead of the vague pronouncements of righteousness and evil.

CHAPTER 70

Questioning the Inspiration of the Bible

FOR MANY CENTURIES, PEOPLE HAVE been using the Bible as a guide for their everyday lives. Some parts of the Bible are undeniably comforting, instructive, and inspiring, such as many of the Psalms and Proverbs, the stories of Jesus, and much of the advice that Paul wrote to the early churches. However, considering the Bible as a whole, there are also many passages that give bad examples or poor advice. For instance, God instructing the Israelites to kill every man, woman, and child in Jericho (Joshua 6:17). And there was the recommendation for stoning to death a rebellious son (Deuteronomy 21:18–21). Adulterers were also commanded to be put to death (Leviticus 20:10). So were witches (Exodus 22:18).

In many churches, the Bible is called the Word of God. It is a collection of books written many centuries ago by men who are considered to have been inspired by God. If the Bible is really the true Word of God, more important than any messages that have been received or written in the intervening centuries, this raises some important questions.

First, how did the Bible come to be considered the Word of God? How did the Bible get to the status of Sacred Scripture? Somehow this odd collection of old writings came to be venerated and exalted above what anyone else said and sometimes even above common sense. How did that happen?

I don't know how the original decisions were made to venerate certain writings and call them the Word of God, but the fact that so many people have unthinkingly continued to consider the Bible to be the Word of God leads me to suspect some kind of mass hypnosis. After all, when a child hears the Bible consistently referred to as "the Word of God," he or she tends to believe that it really is the word of God (unless he or she stops to question this supposition and go against what everyone else is saying). I am convinced that most people who read the Bible or who hear it in church don't really think about the words, at least not very much. If they did, there would be a lot more discussion, a lot more pushback, and probably a lot more arguing.

Once, years ago, I made an appointment with a highly regarded minister to ask him how the Bible got to be so important. He impressed on me that the Bible was originally copied by hand very carefully and also had been translated with extreme care. That completely failed to answer my most basic question. The Bible that was copied and translated—how did that particular set of writings come to be considered sacred? How did it gain the status of being called the Word of God?

If the Bible is really the Word of God, why did God speak to men in ancient times and then stop speaking to people many centuries ago? Certainly God has the ability to speak, and at least a few people have the ability to listen. So if God has not spoken to anyone, it must be because God chooses not to.

Why would God give us God's Word in a form that is confusing, contradictory, and often unbelievable? How are people supposed to understand and live by the often ambiguous or even contradictory words of the Bible?

If God spoke to the writers of the Bible, what stops God from speaking to us today? Why can't God just talk to us in the way people talk to each other? It can't be that hard for God!

Or is it possible that at least some of the Bible is simply a creation of man's imagination? I believe that there is evidence not only that the Bible was written by men but also that the God of the Bible (especially the Old Testament) was created in the image of man!

I can imagine that it might have happened this way: In the beginning of the Bible, men created a God who was like them—patriarchal, vengeful, prejudiced, misogynistic, and having his favorites, while having little respect for anyone who was not part of the chosen group.

They sought to remove all traces of the matriarchal society and goddess worship that had preceded their patriarchal religion. In earlier times, and even continuing among some of the other tribes in the region, people worshipped a goddess who symbolized fertility, peace, and cooperation. In matriarchal society, women had all the political power, and men had very little authority. After patriarchal religion took over, men invented a male god who gave men all the power and who indulged them in their war games.

The god they invented bore only a little resemblance to the One True God. But it was the best they could come up with, and they tried mightily to keep their people worshipping that God, while they sought to eradicate all vestiges of goddess worship.

Even so, occasionally the worship of Ashtorath or other goddesses is mentioned in the Bible. The most notable example is King Solomon, who had seven hundred wives and three hundred concubines (an extreme example of polygamy!). Some of his wives turned Solomon toward the worship of Ashtorath, the goddess of the Sidonians (1 Kings 11:3–5).

I believe that there are many examples of prophets and biblical writers who were divinely inspired, but I also believe that the inspiration was often tainted by their patriarchal biases.

CHAPTER 71

More Questions about the Bible

THESE ARE SOME OF THE other questions I have had about the Bible:

- Was it really God who inspired the writers of the Bible?
- If God spoke to the writers of the Bible, why did God stop talking to people?
- Or if God has continued to inspire and talk to people, why do we cling to that old and often confusing text?
- How could the One God of the Universe choose one small group of people as His Chosen People?
- Why would God insist on circumcision of males? (On this subject, I am very glad that He tended to ignore females!)
- Why do we rely on that old set of writings? Why haven't there been any newer Scriptures?
- Does God really intend for us to try, and keep on trying, to understand what the Bible means? Even when it's very confusing?
- Why couldn't Almighty God find a Promised Land that was unoccupied? Was real estate already developed to the point of scarcity?
- Why are women so pointedly ignored in the Bible?
- Is God really male?

CHAPTER 72

What Is Wrong with Me?

ALL THROUGH MY CHILDHOOD AND for decades beyond, I had the persistent sense that there was something fundamentally wrong with me. As an adult, I had the thought that therapy could be helpful to many people, but I believed that my own flaw was so fundamental that even therapy would not be able to help me.

I see now that much of my thinking along this line was my reaction to the Bible. According to my parents, the Bible was a wonderful book, the best ever written, and I was obligated to love and respect it and try to understand what it was telling me.

I questioned myself endlessly. Why do I not love this story? What am I missing? Why doesn't this make sense to me? What is wrong with me that I do not love and understand and cherish the Word of God? I believed that God would punish me for not loving and cherishing His Word. But even when I puzzled over stories and verses from the Bible, I could rarely see them in a positive light.

And because my parents and all of their friends seemed to have such a high regard for the Bible, I concluded that there was something wrong with my understanding of the Bible—and especially with my emotional response to it. I thought that I was the only person who had a problem with it because I didn't hear anyone asking the questions that I kept hidden away in my mind.

Thinking about it now, I can wonder what was wrong with everyone else that they were unable to perceive the horrors of wrathful actions by God and the inconsistencies in the Bible.

CHAPTER 73

Alternative Versions of the Bible

HAVING HEARD AND/OR READ THE Bible all my life, I occasionally like to amuse myself by making up alternative forms of Bible stories. For instance:

"Adam's Companion"

The Bible says that, after God created the world and everything in it, he formed Adam from the dust of the ground and breathed into his nostrils the breath of life. Then God said, "It is not good that the man should be alone. I will make a helper fit for him." So God formed every beast of the field and every bird of the air and brought them to the man. There was not found a helper fit for him, so God caused Adam to fall into a deep sleep and formed a woman from one of his ribs. Then Adam said, "This is now bone of my bone and flesh of my flesh." He thus accepted the woman as his helper. (Genesis 2:18–23)

This story arouses my suspicions. It sounds as though God expected Adam to choose an animal as his "helper." And when Adam had rejected every one of them, God gave a deep sigh and reluctantly made a woman, possibly with the thought, You have no idea what kind of trouble you're getting yourself into. The writer of Genesis made sure that the woman was created from a small portion of the man's body, making her subservient to the man right from the start.

There could have been a different ending to the story. What if, while God was presenting each animal to Adam,

God introduced him to the dog. In a stunning moment of recognition, Adam and the dog looked at each other with soulful eyes, and Adam said, "Aha! This lovely animal will be my companion and playmate. I will call him dog. Thank you, God!"

Then Adam and his dog proceeded to romp joyously together through the garden of Eden. The two were inseparable, and they never needed anyone else. And God never had to go through the messy and troublesome business of creating woman and the possibility of generation upon generation of sinful human beings.

The end. (The rest of the Bible didn't have to be written!)

***

Because the Bible is written with an overwhelming bias toward men, I also like to imagine the Bible with gender roles reversed. Here are excerpts from:

"The Goddess Bible"

In the beginning, Goddess created the heaven and the earth. And Goddess formed woman of the dust of the ground and breathed into her nostrils the breath of life, and Eve became a living soul. And Goddess said, "It is not good that woman should be alone; I will make a companion for her." And Goddess caused a deep sleep to fall upon Eve, and Goddess took one of her ribs and made a man and brought him unto the woman. And Eve said, "This is now bone of my bone, and flesh of my flesh; and he shall be called Man, because he was taken out of Woman."

***

Many people were born to populate the earth, and Goddess saw that the wickedness of people was great upon the earth. And Goddess said, "I will destroy both human beings and beasts of the earth." But Norah found grace in the eyes of Goddess. And Goddess told Norah to build an ark. So Norah built the ark and gathered food for all the living things and gathered a pair of each kind of beast into the ark. Norah and her (unnamed) husband, and her daughters Sheila, Helen, and Judith and their (unnamed) husbands all entered the ark and shut the door.

Then Goddess caused rain to fall upon the earth for forty days and forty nights, and all living things were destroyed. After many more days, all the inhabitants of the ark walked out on dry land. And Goddess placed a rainbow in the sky and made a covenant with the people that She would never again send a flood to destroy all flesh.

***

There was a righteous woman named Sarah. Sarah and her husband Abraham had no children. For many years she kept hoping to have a child, but she did not conceive. One day, Goddess sent three visitors unto Sarah, and they told her that she and Abraham would have a daughter.

Abraham, listening behind the door of the tent, laughed, saying, "Sarah is old, and I am so old that I can just barely get it up. How can we have a daughter in our old age?"

However, it came to pass as the visitors foretold. A daughter named Isabel was born to Sarah and Abraham.

***

When the people of the Goddess were enslaved in Egypt, they cried out to Goddess to release them from their bondage. Goddess commanded Miriam to lead her people out of Egypt. Miriam led them through the Red Sea. And when they were safely on the other side, her brother Moses danced for joy.

Miriam then led her people through the wilderness in a very short time, as she was willing to ask for directions. When they arrived at the Promised Land, the Israelites were delighted to see that Goddess had led them to a beautiful land, empty and just waiting for them!

***

When the time was right, Goddess sent Her daughter Jessica to save Her people. Jessica the Christ walked among the people and taught them and healed them. Many people listened to her and rejoiced, saying, "This is the one we have been waiting for!"

When some people turned against Jessica and killed her, she responded by rising from the dead and appearing to the group of twelve women who were her followers.

***

The apostle Paula traveled extensively to tell people about Jessica Christ. She also wrote letters telling church members how to behave: "Let your men keep silence in the churches, for it is not permitted unto them to speak; but they are commanded to be under obedience, according to the law. And if they will learn anything, let them ask their wives at home, for it is a shame for men to speak in the church. Let the man learn in silence with all subjection. I do not permit a man to teach, nor to usurp authority over the woman, but to be in silence. For Eve was first formed, then Adam. And Eve was not deceived, but the man was deceived and became the transgressor. Notwithstanding, he shall be saved by begetting offspring, if he continues in faith and charity and holiness with sobriety" (paraphrase of 1 Corinthians 14:34 and 1 Timothy 11–15).

I'm not sure that replacing God-with-a-penis with God-with-a-vagina is really helpful. But I had fun with it!

CHAPTER 74

Finding My Way, Again

A FTER EIGHTEEN YEARS OF PRACTICING Sahaj Marg meditation, when I decided it didn't fit my needs anymore, I felt like I was once again drifting, without an anchor, without a destination. I didn't know where I was going. I appreciated the freedom from participating in a practice that no longer felt good to me, but I had nothing to replace it with.

I was attracted to the writings of Neale Donald Walsch, his Conversations with God and other writings. I felt encouraged and uplifted by reading the conversations between this very human man and Almighty God, who engaged in conversation with him with patience and humor and occasionally some startling insights. This was a God who was very accessible and understanding. A very kind and loving God, Walsch's God was without a trace of the judgment and condemnation that I had come to associate with God. I felt joy and a sense of relief just contemplating a God of pure love.

I was also fascinated to read about the experiences of people who had died and then were resuscitated and who remembered what happened to them while they were "dead." Most of the people who had those experiences had no connection or knowledge of other people who had near-death experiences. However, most of their stories were remarkably similar in their descriptions of feeling loved and understood in ways that were infinitely more comforting and profound than they had ever experienced in their regular life. This encouraged me to consider the possibility that the portrayal of God in the Bible is very far from being the Truth about God.

Recently, I have once again become interested in studying A Course in Miracles. Earlier in my adult life, I had studied it diligently for about ten years, and I had given up on it because I had difficulty practicing the exercises. I also had no support for my practice at that time. But now, thirty years later, I have found many helpful websites on the internet. I also got in touch with a small group of women who study the course together locally. So I have come back to studying the Course, and I am determined to continue for the foreseeable future.

CHAPTER 75

Getting Over the Bible

AS A CHILD, I WAS told in many ways that the Bible was the precious Word of God. I was expected to listen to it, read it as I became able to read, and eventually study it carefully. I was also told that I was obligated to love the God who was portrayed in the Bible. I really wanted to please my parents and teachers, so I listened to daily Bible reading even though I didn't like it most of the time. There was much in it that I didn't understand, and there were some things that horrified me.

But when I was told that I was required to love the God of the Bible, I knew that was impossible for me. I knew that adults often did things that I didn't consider enjoyable, such as sitting quietly during long, boring church services; being serious instead of being playful; eating bad-smelling vegetables without complaining; and working very long and hard on tasks that I didn't understand. I accepted those things as being part of the mysterious life of adults. But I could not begin to understand how they could love a God who demanded impossibly high standards of behavior and was usually threatening to punish or destroy people because of their wickedness.

All the adults around me—the minister of our church, my teachers at school and Sunday school, and my parents and their friends—treated the Bible with great respect and honor. We had relatives who lived on farms and had hardly any books in their homes, but each had a Bible and read out loud from the Bible every day. I felt great pressure from the adults around me to love and appreciate the Bible as much as they did.

Even though I could not find a way to appreciate much of that highly rated book, and I absolutely could not love bad-tempered God, I continued to feel daily pressure to read and listen to the Bible. I resented the importance placed on that book, and internally, I fought against the pressure to believe what the Bible taught. But the pressure was continuous, and I felt very much alone in my dislike of the Bible, as everyone around me seemed to think it was a very wonderful book.

I also believed that many of my problems were related to the Bible. I believed that my shyness and social awkwardness and questioning my own worth were related to the emphasis I heard from the Bible about righteousness and the perils of sinfulness. I was tense and nervous and had trouble sleeping because I believed that, no matter how hard I tried, I would never be able to come close to living up to the standard that the Bible set for me. I also was constantly preoccupied with trying to understand and accept things that I couldn't understand, especially how the alleged "goodness of God" was in any way related to the mean, scary God I had always been hearing about. I believed that I was a poor miserable sinner, and I continued to have sinful thoughts and actions all the time. I could hardly go one minute without having thoughts of pride or resentment or revenge. And not a day went by that I didn't do or say something I considered sinful. I believed that God would punish me for my sins.

I desperately wanted to be comforted, but I had nobody to turn to for the comfort and reassurance that I craved. My parents were always quick to point out my faults. They wanted me to be a perfect Christian child, and I was unable to fulfill their wishes. I definitely could not rely on Big Bad God. So I took what comfort I could in my books and my dolls and playing the piano. Because my desire for comfort and reassurance was thwarted, I was often sullen and moody. My sister Ruth, as a young child, had expressed her needs by being defiant. And when punishment didn't help to change her behavior, my parents decided that she needed more love. That was helpful for her. I could have used more love, too, but I didn't know how to ask for it.

As an adult, I have spent decades thinking about all the harm the Bible has done. It has given us a description of an angry, jealous, murderous, misogynistic, prejudiced God who sometimes helps his favorites but also demands extremely high standards of behavior and is constantly disappointed when his chosen people do not meet those standards. Although the Psalms describe God as "kind and merciful, slow to anger and abounding in steadfast love" (Psalm 103) and insists that, "The Lord is good; his steadfast love endures forever, and his faithfulness to all generations" (Psalm 99), many of the actions of God described in the Bible consist of demands or threats or acts of destruction. It seems to me that the psalmists want to reassure themselves that God is loving and helpful. Or maybe they are trying to tell God how they hope He will behave toward them.

After decades of taking issue with many of the things that are written in the Bible and wishing that it had not had such a prominent place in my life or in the world, I have finally come to a new conclusion: Whatever happened in the past is over. It is time for me, right now, today, to let go of all the hard feelings I have had toward the Bible. Not because the Bible needs it, but because I need it! I've been blaming the Bible, but actually I've been doing it to myself!

I am free to believe what I find believable and what makes sense to me. I am free to accept what feels good and right. And if other people want to believe ideas that don't appeal to me, they are free to believe whatever they want.

Ultimately, the truth is true! Just because millions of people believe something (or try to believe it!) doesn't mean that it is true. I no longer have to contort myself to try to believe ideas that don't make sense to me. What a relief!

CHAPTER 76

Goodbye to Big, Bad, Scary God

W HEN I LOOK AT THE main stories of the Bible, it is no wonder that I used to consider God to be mean and scary. After creating the world—a stunning, amazing feat—and creating the animals, He created a man. All good so far.

Then, when the man wanted a companion, God made a woman out of the man's rib. Uh-oh. There is something different about this. Instead of directly creating the woman, God uses a part of the already-created man to form the woman, thus signifying that she is not directly created by God in the same way as the man. She is apparently made from the man for the man.

God turns them loose to enjoy the garden but tells them not to eat of the fruit of one tree. Didn't He even know that He had created people who were curious and who sometimes did what they were told not to do?

After the man and the woman ate the forbidden fruit (which He certainly could have predicted!) God banished them from the garden and sentenced them to a lifetime of hard work and pain. He didn't tell them He was sorry He had to do it; He just kicked them out, and that was that.

Thereafter, throughout the Old Testament, God is mostly noticing evildoing and punishing or destroying evildoers. He does that in the time of Noah, destroying the whole of evil humankind, all except Noah's family. He dramatically destroys the wicked cities of Sodom and Gomorrah with fire and brimstone. He gives the Israelites hundreds of rules for them to obey so that they can be truly righteous.

But human beings keep on thinking evil thoughts and committing evil deeds. So eventually God sends his only-begotten Son and requires

267

him to be tortured and killed as a way of making amends for the unending sins of humankind.

Something about this makes no sense. It's not even logical. If God created human beings with the tendencies toward thoughts and behaviors that they have, why would God be dismayed when people think and act the way they were created to think and act? Was God unaware of what kind of people He had created? Some people have explained that God gave us free will. If we choose the right way, we will be rewarded, and if we choose the wrong way, we will be punished. That doesn't sound like free will to me. Rather, it seems a test to see who will do what they're supposed to do, and to hell (literally!) with everyone else.

I have not found anything warm and fuzzy about that God. That is the God that I believed was always watching me, examining my thoughts and actions disapprovingly, and making note of all my evil thoughts and bad deeds. Of course I did not want to go to heaven to sit in front of Big, Bad, Scary, Judgmental God! Why would anyone in his or her right mind choose to spend eternity in the presence of the Supreme Judge, who was making note of all our thoughts and actions and finding fault with most of them? That is the most uncomfortable thing I can imagine. Of course I kept hoping to find something better.

Fortunately, very fortunately, I have learned that the wrathful, judgmental, angry God is not the real God. The Course in Miracles shows us a God of pure love, a God who is love, and we are all part of that love. Our unloving and fearful thoughts are not real; only the thoughts that we think with God (love) are real. The real God does not condemn. He only loves.

According to the Course, we are actually safe and happy in heaven with God right now. There has never been any separation, and we are only dreaming this world, which does not really exist. Of course, this is very hard for us to believe because our bodies, the world, and all the stuff in it seem absolutely real and solid to our senses. But in the universe of the real God, contrary to what we may believe, everything that exists is an expression of perfect love, and we are holy children of God, reflecting the splendor of our Father.

The Course in Miracles is designed to help us undo all the false ideas we have about ourselves and to undo what the ego has made. Ultimately, we will be able to completely accept ourselves—and everyone else—as holy children of God. In actuality, we are all joined together in perfect love and unity; sin and guilt do not exist.

Of course it is not easy for us to understand and believe that, which is why the course gives us 365 daily lessons to practice and more than six hundred pages of text to study. And we are expected to actually do the work. Our main assignment is forgiveness—that is, recognizing that all the grudges and grievances we hold against people are mistaken and letting go of them. In fact, that is how we are saved. The Course teaches us how to change our minds and let go of the false beliefs we have had about ourselves and everyone else. And we have very many false beliefs. By going through this process, we become progressively clearer and happier and more loving. It is definitely worth the effort!

The more I study the Course, the more I feel connected to God. Instead of seeing the bad-tempered, unpredictable old man in the sky, I am more and more perceiving God as pure love. This is a God who only loves, who connects to all His children, and finds no fault with any of them because they—we—are all His beloved children. And we have never, ever done anything to cause Him displeasure (no matter what we think that we—or some of our brothers and sisters—have done). God does not need to forgive us because there is nothing to forgive. It is we who need to forgive ourselves and each other for pain we seem to have caused each other.

To help us on our way, in every moment, we have Jesus and the Holy Spirit who are in constant contact with us. All we need to do is ask and listen and pay attention to what they tell us.

Some people have dismissed A Course in Miracles as a cult or false teachings meant to lead people astray from the "truth" of the Bible. However, for me, even if it is not the ultimate truth, I feel ever so much happier when I think of God as pure love and when I think that all people (my brothers and sisters who are all children of God) are joined together with me in glorious, happy unity. Do I prefer this God of Perfect Love to the old wrathful God who watches all his children fighting with each other, just waiting to catch them doing something wrong? You bet I do! There is really no comparison. I definitely want to choose love rather than fear—just because it feels good!—not only for me but also for every person I encounter.

It is not easy for me to transition from the "God" of fear to the God of love. Certainly many parts of the "Word of God" (the Bible) have not been helpful to me. But the God of love feels infinitely better than the mean, scary, punitive "god" I believed in for so many years. It is definitely worth whatever I need to do to banish Him from my mind.

I can hardly believe my good fortune. It's better than good—a million times better! Rather than fearing Big Bad God, as I did for so many years, I have discovered God Who is Pure Love—who accepts everyone and everything and does not condemn or judge. This is a most dramatic contrast. And I feel completely justified for hating and fearing Big Bad God all these years; he is not the real God, and he does not deserve worship or love. Amen. Hallelujah!

CHAPTER 77

A Course in Miracles

THERE IS A FASCINATING STORY behind A Course in Miracles. One day in June 1965, a psychologist named Bill Thetford, having grown tired of the constant fighting and bickering in his department at Columbia University in New York City, said to his coworker, Helen Schucman, "There must be a better way, and I'm determined to find it." She, very uncharacteristically, agreed to join him in seeking a better way, and they began to find more positive ways to deal with departmental issues.

Meanwhile, Helen began having dreams and visions of a spiritual nature, which surprised her, as she considered herself an atheist. Then, one evening in October, a "voiceless Voice" told her she was going to write a course in miracles and please take notes. Day after day, she took notes given to her by the Voice, sometimes reluctantly and with great resistance, but she persevered.

Bill carefully typed up her notes every day and supported Helen in her work of receiving and writing down the words she was being given. This continued for seven years, while both were still actively engaged in very demanding careers.

The Voice identified himself as Jesus, and not only dictated the course to Helen but also gave Helen and Bill practical advice and guidance.

They kept the course a closely guarded secret, cautiously sharing it with a few selected friends. Fortunately, Kenneth Wapnick and Judith Skutch joined their circle when the course was complete, and they were able to handle the important job of editing the material and preparing it for publication. It was first published in 1976; I purchased my first copy in 1979 and began studying it right away.

The course begins by saying:

> Nothing real can be threatened.
> Nothing unreal exists.
> Herein lies the peace of God.

A Course in Miracles teaches about love, which is the nature of God and also the nature of God's children (all of us!). The textbook teaches about miracles, which are simply acts of love. It teaches about the true nature of heaven, and it describes life on earth as a dream in which we think we are living. But the real truth is that we have never left our home with God. There is no such thing as sin, although people do make mistakes, which in reality are simply a call for love. When we understand that people around us are calling for love, we can respond appropriately. Much of our task is to learn to forgive, or in truth, eventually, to realize that there is nothing to forgive.

In the text, God is described as supreme, beyond definition, all-loving, and all-creative. God and His real creations are perfect and eternal. According to the course, God did not create the physical world! God would have been cruel indeed to create a world in which people suffer and die, a world in which "acts of God" wreak devastation on millions of people, a world of sadness and insanity. Even though this world seems very, very real to us, we have in fact dreamed it and are continuing to dream it. Eventually, we will wake up and discover that we have been dreaming. We are, in fact, eternally with God in heaven, completely safe and totally enveloped in love.

The workbook, consisting of 365 daily lessons, guides us step by step to help us release our tight hold on the ego. This is not an easy process, because we have invested a great deal of ourselves in carefully constructing our egos. The workbook offers us a way out. We are told that we do not have to understand or agree with or even believe the lessons, but if we do them as prescribed, they will help us let go of the stranglehold our own ego has on us. As a result, we will become happier and filled with the love that is our true birthright. Jesus seems to understand how very strongly we identify ourselves with our self-images, and he guides us through a very gradual process of removing the barriers to love that we have erected. He obviously has a very deep understanding of human psychology and uses many forms of encouragement to help us understand and practice ideas that are foreign to our usual way of thinking.

The daily lessons in the "Workbook for Students" include the following statements:

> I am as God created me.
> I am not a body. I am free.
> I could see peace instead of this.
> There is nothing to fear.

The course also includes a short "Manual for Teachers." He (Jesus, dictating to Helen) makes the point that we are all teachers who are always teaching others by what we say and do.

The ideas in the course, the vast amount of reading material, and the vocabulary used, are obviously intended for well-educated people who have some knowledge of the Bible. This leads me to consider the great variety of spiritual paths in the world. I have come to the conclusion that there are many different paths that fulfill needs of many different people. Sometimes even the same person has different needs at various stages of his or her life. That has certainly been true for me.

I had wished for modern inspiration to take the place of what I considered the outmoded and faulty teachings of the Bible. A Course in Miracles is very practical, very thorough, and seems to be designed specifically for today's people. Several historic events helped to prepare the way for the Course. The theories of Sigmund Freud regarding the id, ego, and superego provide a background for understanding the Course, even though the term ego has a slightly different definition in the course. I believe it is no accident that the Course was transmitted to a psychologist who was well versed in contemporary theories of personality (Helen Schucman) and aided by another psychologist who was a leading expert in the development of the ego (Bill Thetford).

I also think that it is no coincidence that the transmission started in 1965, the same year that the Catholic Church was going through significant changes. With the changes made in the Vatican II conference,

Pope John XXIII made it acceptable for Catholics to join with people of other faiths, thus ushering in a new age of ecumenism. This helped people open up to new sources of inspiration.

I am indeed grateful for A Course in Miracles, which offers me precise instructions and help to find my way out of the illusory world of pain and struggle in which I seem to be ensnared, and into the state of eternal love and bliss that is my true birthright.

CHAPTER 78

God Did Not Create This World

HERE IS THE ANSWER TO so many questions that people have been asking for centuries: Why did God create a world of sadness, sickness, and death; a world of struggle and competition; a world of famine and violent storms; and a world in which people compete with each other and even kill each other? We have looked for answers. We have pleaded for help from the God who made it all, often with no satisfaction. Because of that, some people have decided that God does not exist or, if God existed at some time, God is now dead.

However, the truth—as put forth in A Course in Miracles, and which feels absolutely true to me—is that God did not create this world of hardships and suffering. In reality this world does not exist. God is perfect and eternal, and what He creates is perfect and eternal, including His children. We are dreaming this world and have not awakened from the dream. Because we are so thoroughly invested in our version of the dream, it is necessary to go through a process of forgiveness in order to let go. Forgiveness really means coming to the realization that we are completely innocent and have done no wrong, and everyone else is equally innocent and holy. That is difficult from our perspective because it's obvious that people have injured and even killed each other. However, as much as we identify with our bodies, we are not our bodies. The true essence of ourselves cannot be harmed in any way. A Course in Miracles says that every action is either an act of love or a call for love; thus, any action that seems unloving can be interpreted as a call for love.

How did this world of separation get started? In one instant a "tiny, mad idea" of separation crept in, and the unified, holy Son of God forgot to laugh! (Course in Miracles, chapter 27). By taking the idea seriously, the entire dream network of the world was formed. I imagine that it might have been something like this:

"How the World Was Made"

There They were, all blissfully together in the ever-expanding moment of now, full of love and joy in the Kingdom of Heaven. A fleeting thought came to one of Them: What would it be like if we were all separate individuals? It was a most ridiculous idea, but the moment he forgot to laugh, his thought created a big bang (although it was still in his imagination) and this imaginary, although seemingly solid, world became manifest.

What fun he had playing with physical matter on the big ball—building hills and mountains and even bigger mountains, stirring up the water in the oceans, rolling boulders around, and crunching grains of sand! There were all kinds of new experiences here. There were high and low, wet and dry, hot and cold, smooth and rough, large and small, fast and slow—opposites that were not part of the Kingdom of Heaven, where all is peace and joy and bliss without any opposite.

He imagined living things into being—all sorts of plants and animals. Although these were apparently alive, they were temporary. That is to say, each had a beginning and an end, unlike the eternal spirits in the real world of heaven. His imagination went wild, thinking up all sorts of plants—moss and grass and trees and cactus and flowering bushes—all with their own characteristics. He also imagined organisms that were not attached to the ground. There were insects that flew or crawled, snakes that slithered, fish of all sizes that swam in the water, birds that flew in the air, and a fantastic array of animals. He envisioned monkeys, giraffes, elephants, horses, dogs, and tigers, to name a few.

And for a while, he played with dinosaurs but let them disappear, as something even more interesting began to happen: Many of the souls from heaven came to experience life on earth as human beings.

Human beings came in separate packages called bodies, and each body had needs for nourishment and warmth and interaction with other bodies. Many had difficulty adjusting to the heavy conditions of earth—in stark contrast to heaven, where all is peace and joy and light and where every place is here and every time is now.

Things started to happen that could never have happened in heaven. People competed with each other, fighting and even killing each other's bodies. People developed an exaggerated sense of distinctiveness and separation from each other. "I," "me," and "mine" were some of their favorite words, with each one trying to establish his or her own superiority and the inferiority of others. They experienced fear, which was new to them, as in heaven there was only love, with no opposite. People forgot their heavenly origin and began to think that their bodies were their real selves. None of this was actually true, but during their temporary stay on earth, they were absolutely convinced that it was.

Meanwhile, back in Heaven, God blissfully continues to share his inexhaustible love with His holy children, not even noticing that many of them imagine that they are participating in an earthly experiment, which is not real but certainly feels real to them.

And it feels real to us, God's holy children, who seem to be caught up in a physical "reality," not realizing that it is only a dream, and we are actually safe in heaven and have never left the loving abundance of God. As we return to the secure presence of God, we can all enjoy happy laughter about our dream of separation.

CHAPTER 79

The Message of A Course in Miracles

A COURSE IN MIRACLES IS MAINLY about forgiveness. It says, in Lesson 99, "Your Father loves you. All the world of pain is not His will. Forgive yourself the thought He wanted this for you … Open your secrets to His kindly light, and see how bright this light still shines in you today."

As every student of the Course soon discovers, forgiveness may be simple, but it is far from easy. There seems to be no end to the judgmental, angry, unloving thoughts we have. As we uncover some that we didn't know we had, we discover that there are more there. It can seem like an endless task. However, as we continue to let go of unloving, judgmental thoughts, we become lighter and happier. And as we reap the rewards of practicing the Course, we become even more motivated to keep doing it.

According to our egos, we have separated ourselves from God. We believe this is a sin. And through our guilt, we believe that we deserve God's punishment. However, most of our guilt is unconscious. Even though it is unconscious, it still affects us and makes us fearful. In fact, our most common strategy is to deny guilt in ourselves and project it onto someone else, thus believing someone else is guilty and we are innocent. Through our forgiveness, which we direct toward others but which we actually need for ourselves, we gradually uncover and release the guilt that has been pulling us down.

The "miracles" spoken of in A Course in Miracles are not the seemingly supernatural events we tend to think of as miracles, such as raising the dead, healing the sick, and restoring sight to the blind. Rather, each miracle naturally reveals the love that was hidden behind judgmental or fearful thoughts. As the Course says, "Miracles are natural. When they do not occur something has gone wrong" (Text, Chapter 1).

God really wants us to be completely happy! And we cannot be completely happy while we are harboring fearful, angry, judgmental thoughts. The Course asks, "Would you rather be happy or be right?" So often we have such a strong need to hold on to our opinion rather than allow Truth to be revealed to us that we make ourselves unhappy. However, we really can be happy if we let go and allow love to take the place of fear.

One aspect of A Course in Miracles that I especially appreciate is the generous attitude summed up in these statements: "To give and to receive are one in truth" (W108). "I trust my brothers who are one with me" (W181). "I bless the world because I bless myself" (W187). And the final lesson in the workbook is:

> Peace be to me, the holy Son of God
> Peace to my brother, who is one with me.
> Let all the world be blessed with peace through us.

I love this attitude of cooperation and mutual help, so different from the competition and struggle we encounter in our world.

I will end my writing with this heartfelt prayer from A Course in Miracles:

> Forgive us our illusions, Father,
> and help us to accept our true relationship with You,
> in which there are no illusions, and where none can ever enter.
> Our holiness is Yours.
> What can there be in us that needs forgiveness when Yours is perfect?
> The sleep of forgetfulness is only the unwillingness to remember
> Your forgiveness and Your Love.
> Let us not wander into temptation,
> for the temptation of the Son of God is not your Will.

And let us receive only what You have given
and accept but this into the minds which
You created and which You love.
Amen.

(from the end of Chapter 16 in the Text)

Printed in the United States
by Baker & Taylor Publisher Services